Christmas 91

To a proud veteran of one
era from a proud veteran of
another. Airborne, All the way
"De Oppresso Libre"

Dave

WAR IN KOREA

BY THE SAME AUTHOR

Roosevelt, de Gaulle and the Posts
Franco-American War Relations Viewed Through
Their Effects on the French Postal System,
1942-1944

Airbridge to Berlin
The Berlin Crisis of 1948,
its Origins and Aftermath
(with Robert E. Griffin)

WAR
IN
KOREA
1950-1953

D. M. GIANGRECO

PRESIDIO

Printed in the United States of America by Ringier
America, Inc. of Olathe Kansas. Type by Lopez
Graphics, Inc. of Kansas City, Missouri.

Library of Congress Cataloging-in-Publication Data

Giangreco, D. M., 1952–
    War in Korea, 1950-1953: a pictorial history / D. M. Giangreco.
        p.   cm.
    ISBN 0-89141-379-0
    1. Korean War, 1950-1953—Pictorial works.   I. Title.
DS918.15.G53
951.904'2–dc20   90-7187
                                                  CIP

Quality printing and binding by
  Ringier America, Inc.
  2115 E. Kansas City Road
  Olathe, Kansas 66061
  U.S.A.

to Lieutenant Colonel Roy E. Appleman (Ret.)
for his untiring effort
to chronicle the Korean War

Preface

On Sunday, 25 June 1950, seven North Korean divisions supported by tanks and aircraft invaded the southern Republic of Korea. Three years and over five million casualties later, an armistice ended the fighting only miles from where it had begun.

Vastly smaller in scale than the Second World War and pushed into the background of our nation's consciousness by the prolonged trauma of Vietnam, the Korean War has become little more than a footnote in history to most Americans. But to the one and a half million US fighting men who served in that short, vicious, "police action," their struggle to contain Communist aggression was no less a war than any other fought in our nation's history. Memories of the endless hostile hills, gritty pudding-like mud, snow and choking dust, the long periods of boredom and violent death of friends still linger in the minds of those who fought there.

After the Second World War, it had been widely assumed by pundits and public alike that the next conflict would be a "push-button" atomic war where the individual mattered little. Any suggestion that within a few short years US soldiers and Marines would be peering across a no man's land from behind barriers of dirt, land mines and barbed wire would have seemed laughable; an impossible throwback to the trench warfare of 1918 when doughboys dug deep into French fields to escape the Kaiser's bullets. In Korea, the fighting was often hand-to-hand. A bayonet and a few grenades could decide whether you lived or died and your best friends on earth were your M-1 Garand rifle, a shovel and your buddy in the next foxhole.

Contained on these pages are 521 of the countless thousands of photographs taken during the Korean War. They cover not only Army and Marine ground forces, but also the vitally important operations carried out by the US Navy and Air Force, as well as the troops of Great Britain, Turkey, Australia and other nations serving under the United Nations' flag. Shot almost exclusively by military photographers, they are frozen instants in a war that is now largely forgotten. My intent in publishing these pictures is to promote further study of this conflict; a limited war which did not satisfy the traditional need of Americans to revel in rapid and total victory, yet did manage to preserve the independence of one small Asian nation.

D. M. Giangreco
Kansas City, Missouri
23 April 1990

Acknowledgments

I would like to thank the many people whose kind assistance made this book possible. Among those who helped me locate photographs for *War in Korea* are Mary Beth Straight and Linda Cullen of the US Naval Institute; Colonel John E. Greenwood, US Marine Corps (Ret.) and Master Sergeant Joseph D. Dodd, US Marine Corps (Ret.) of the *Marine Corps Gazette*; Monica Butler of the United Nation's Photo Library; John Westcott and Steve Garst of *Airpower Journal*, the professional journal of the US Air Force; Pauline Testerman of the Harry S. Truman Library; Fred Pernell of the National Archives, Still Pictures Branch; Betty Bohannon and Carol Ramkey of the US Army Command and General Staff College Library; Mike Bucannon of the 1361st Audio Visual Squadron, US Air Force; Commander William P. Davis, US Navy (Ret.) of the Chosin Few veteran's organization; Melissa Keiser of the National Air and Space Museum; and Colonel David H. Hackworth, US Army (Ret.).

A number of serving and retired officers also gave generously of their time to assist me with the production of this book and showed remarkable patience in answering my many questions: Colonel Franklin B. Nihart, US Marine Corps (Ret.) and Brigadier General Edwin H. Simmons, US Marine Corps (Ret.) of the Marine Corps Historical Center, both of whom fought in actions outlined on these pages; Captain Shelby L. Stanton, US Army (Ret.); and, from the US Army's professional journal, *Military Review*, Colonel Philip W. Childress, Major Chris J. LeBlanc, Major José H. Rivera and Captain John M. Powell. Other *Military Review* staffers, Cynthia L. Teare and Margaret M. Blue, provided invaluable assistance by reviewing and proofreading the text as did Kathy Moore.

In thanking all those who provided their help so freely I should also add that any errors in this book are solely my responsibility.

Contents

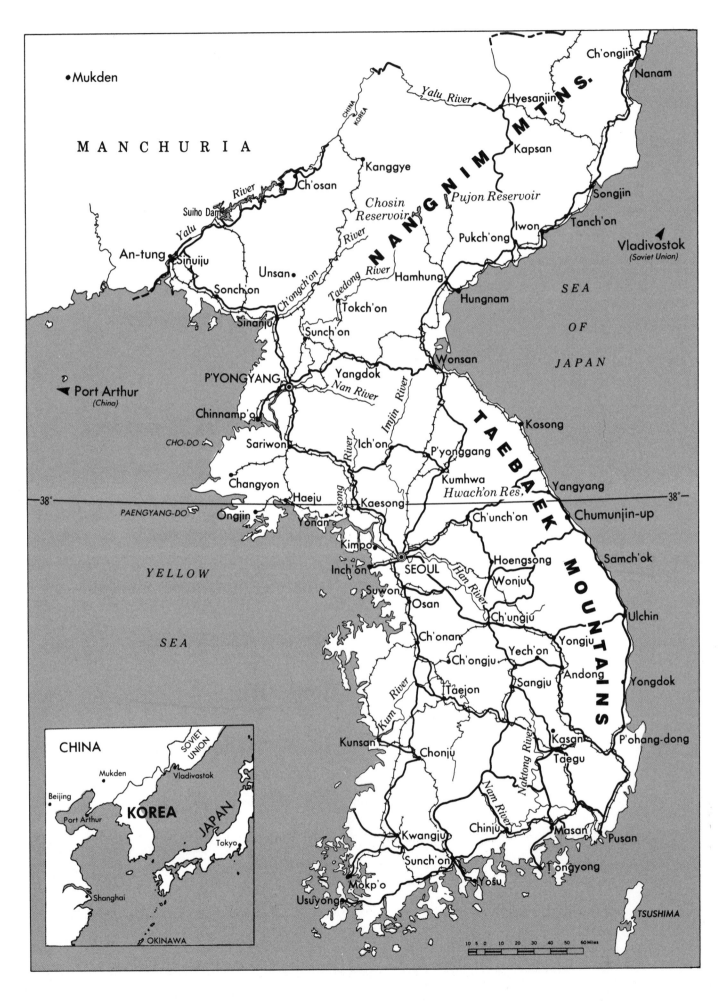

Mukden

MANCHURIA

Yalu River

Ch'ongjin

Nanam

Hyesanjin

NANGNIM MTNS.

Kapsan

Kanggye

Ch'osan

River

Chosin Reservoir

Pujon Reservoir

Songjin

Suiho Dam

Yalu

Iwon

Tanch'on

Vladivostok
(Soviet Union)

An-tung

Sinuiju

Unsan

Pukch'ong

Sonch'on

River

Taedong River

Hamhung

SEA

Ch'ongch'on

Sinanju

Tokch'on

Hungnam

OF

Sunch'on

JAPAN

Wonsan

Port Arthur
(China)

P'YONGYANG

Yangdok

Nan River

Imjin River

Chinnamp'o

Kosong

CHO-DO

Sariwon

Ich'on

P'yonggang

Changyon

River

Kumhwa

Yangyang

Hwach'on Res.

38°

Haeju

Kaesong

38°

PAENGYANG-DO

Ongjin

Yonan

Yesong

Chumunjin-up

Ch'unch'on

Kimpo

Hoengsong

Samch'ok

Inch'on

SEOUL

Wonju

Suwon

Han River

Ch'ungju

Ulchin

YELLOW

Osan

Ch'onan

Yongju

SEA

Yech'on

Andong

Ch'ongju

Yongdok

Sangju

Taejon

Kum

Kasan

Kunsan

River

P'ohang-dong

Chonju

Taegu

Nam River

Naktong River

Chinju

Masan

Pusan

Kwangju

T'ongyong

Sunch'on

Mokp'o

Yosu

Usuyong

TSUSHIMA

TAEBAEK MOUNTAINS

CHINA

SOVIET UNION

Mukden

Vladivostok

Beijing

KOREA

JAPAN

Port Arthur

Tokyo

Shanghai

OKINAWA

10 5 0   10   20   30   40   50   60 Miles

1

CHAPTER ONE

Korea
A Nation Divided

The Americans who fought in Korea found themselves in a land dominated by mountainous terrain throughout its length. Korea is roughly the size of California south of San Francisco or Italy north of Naples. It enjoys the pleasant climate of neither. The main uplift of the mountains extends along the entire east coast of the peninsula and gradually yields to regions of low rolling hills and valleys dotted with rice paddies in the west. There are no thick forests anywhere in Korea and the only vegetation that can be found clinging to its rocky slopes are sparse grasses peppered with stunted trees and small bushes. Winters are bitterly cold and the summer monsoons of the early 1950s turned the country's few dirt roads into quagmires.

Throughout its long, sad history, Korea has suffered numerous invasions. First the Japanese and, later, both the Japanese and the Russians fought for possession of the peninsula's strategically located ports to support their imperial aims on China. Japan finally gained complete control of the peninsula in 1910 and immediately embarked on a campaign to eradicate all vestiges of Korea's unique language and culture. The Japanese built roads, factories and docks but, in return, Koreans became third-class citizens in their own country. Shop owners were forced out of business and no Korean was permitted to remain in a government position of any authority. Only the Japanese language could be taught to the few students allowed into grammar schools, the names of Korean cities were changed to their Japanese equivalents and people harboring "dangerous thoughts" were imprisoned.

When World War II came to its sudden and unexpected conclusion with the dropping of atomic bombs on two of Japan's major industrial cities, the United States found itself responsible for the needs of roughly 14 million people in the southern half of Korea. A hurried agreement signed on 15 August 1945, divided the peninsula into US and Soviet occupation zones at the 38th degree of latitude. The "38th Parallel," as it soon came to be known, neatly bisected the country into almost equal halves but did not conform with either provincial boundaries or geographic features as it cut across mountains, valleys and more than 85 rivers and streams.

Korea's situation after hostilities ended presented US occupation forces with a special set of problems. On Okinawa, the XXIV Corps' 6th, 7th and 40th Infantry Divisions, under Lieutenant General John R. Hodge, had just begun training for the projected invasion of Japan when they were told to pack up their tents and get ready for movement to Korea, where they would disarm all Japanese forces below the 38th Parallel. Virtually no political or economic relations had existed between the "Hermit Kingdom" and the United States for decades and the lack of any significant Korean population in the US ensured that State Department and Army efforts to locate Korean-speaking Americans to work as translators would meet with little success.

Ready or not, US forces landed on Saturday, 8 September 1945, six days after Japan's formal surrender, and nearly two weeks after the Soviets had established themselves in the north. What developed was chaos. The short notice meant that almost no preparations had been made for the military occupation and administration of the peninsula. In addition to being understaffed and mostly untrained in its new role, the Military Government had the fundamental handicap of knowing next to nothing about the language and customs of the Korean people, and faced a confused political situation in which dozens of newly formed political parties jockeyed for position. To make matters worse, Hodge turned to the conquered Japanese— for whom he had at least a few interpreters— for administrative help and even said that: "The Korean is the same breed of cats as [the] Japanese."

The outcry raised over Hodge's statement forced him to abandon his use of Korea's ex-overlords and their repatriation to Japan was speeded up. The mad scramble, already underway, to recruit Koreans to assist the Military Government was intensified. It was a touchy situation. The military administration obviously needed help governing this alien land but, at the same time, was under strict orders from Washington not to recognize or utilize "any so-called Korean provisional government or other political organization" since such use might prejudice future elections. Above the 38th Parallel, however, the Soviets openly installed Moscow-schooled Koreans in positions of power and bombarded the population with Communist propaganda.

All efforts by US authorities to establish a unified Korean provisional government were blocked by their Soviet counterparts and the matter was turned over to the United Nations. Communist authorities in the north, however, refused to participate in the UN supervised election of a constituent assembly and, on 10 May 1948, votes were cast only in the southern half of the peninsula. With Moscow's blessing, the Communist Party apparatus, led by Kim Il Sung, formed its own "People's Republic."

The US Military Government formally relinquished power to the newly established Republic of Korea on 15 August 1948 and began withdrawing the last 45,000 occupation troops a month later. Shortly after the start of the troop withdrawals, Communist-inspired revolts erupted and spread rapidly throughout the fledgling republic. Government forces eventually gained the upper hand but it was evident that they did not have the strength to successfully resist a threatened invasion from North Korea.

In November 1948, the South Korean president, Syngman Rhee requested that the US Army, now amounting to only about 16,000 troops, remain until the situation stabilized.

More soldiers were withdrawn but a 7,500-man garrison, made up of the 5th Regimental Combat Team, stayed on through the winter and spring as government forces regained control over the disputed regions. It was finally pulled out with much fanfare in May and June 1949 to coincide with the one year anniversary of the South Korean elections.

A 500-member Military Advisory Group was left behind to supervise the training of the lightly equipped Republic of Korea (ROK) Army, but neither General of the Army Douglas MacArthur, who commanded all US forces in the Far East from his Tokyo headquarters, nor the Joint Chiefs of Staff (JCS) in Washington believed that this force could be made capable of halting a full-scale invasion by the lavishly armed North Korean People's Army (NKPA). As early as 1946, the JCS reported to President Harry S. Truman that in the event of war with the Soviet Union, the XXIV Corps in Korea would have to be pulled back to take part in the defense of Japan. US forces world-wide were stretched so thin after America's post-World War II demobilization that not one of the half dozen major JCS war plans developed prior to 1950 envisioned that the peninsula could be held by the US— let alone by the South Koreans themselves.

In a speech to the National Press Club in January 1950, Secretary of State Dean Acheson stated publicly that the Western defense perimeter of the United States stopped short of South Korea and encompassed only the islands lying off Asia's eastern littoral: Japan, Okinawa and the Philippines. MacArthur also made similar statements during interviews with various daily newspapers, including the *New York Times*, and the same theme was sounded by the chairman of the Senate Foreign Relations Committee, Tom Connally, in May 1950, only a month before the NKPA crossed the 38th Parallel. The Communists could take South Korea with little fear of US intervention, Connally said, because the country wasn't "very greatly important (sic)" to US interests.

To all appearances, the United States was leaving the Republic of Korea to fend for itself in the face of a mounting threat from the North. US leaders in Washington and Tokyo did not believe that the Soviets or their surrogates in North Korea would take advantage of South Korea's weakened state. The Communists, on the other hand, had good reason to expect that they would be given a free hand in invading the South. Such misconceptions would cost both sides dearly.

Soviet forces invaded Manchuria on Thursday, 9 August 1945, the same day that the United States destroyed Nagasaki, Japan, with its second atomic bomb. The nearly one million strong Japanese garrison was quickly defeated and by Sunday, 26 August, elements of the Soviet 25th Army moved almost as far south as the capital of Seoul before retiring to their occupation zone north of the 38th Parallel. US forces disarmed Japanese troops in southern Korea and Japan. (**Above**) US military police stand guard as Japanese soldiers carry rifles, machine guns and swords into a collection point in Yokohama, Japan; (**opposite top**) Soviet troops hitch a ride atop T-34 tanks during the invasion of Manchuria; and (**opposite bottom**) Soviet occupation troops marching along a Korean road.

Saturday, 8 September 1945, the US occupation of southern Korea begins as troops of the 7th Infantry Division land at Inch'on. (**Below**) A young Japanese officer— still armed with his samurai sword— rides along with the crew of an M-8 Greyhound armored car to act as their interpreter.

Joyous students welcome US troops to the Korean capital, 10 September 1945. The caption on this Signal Corps photo called the city Keijo but the students had already discarded the hated Japanese alias in favor of its traditional Korean name. Their banner at right reads: "Welcome! Apostles of Justice U.S.A. Army! We have long awaited for you. Korean Students in Seoul Technical College." (**Below**) Korean police in Pusan march under homemade US and Korean flags to celebrate their liberation on 16 September.

(**Opposite**) Korean peasants transplanting rice shoots and operating a primitive but effective mill. Though the country had long been known as the rice bowl of the Orient because of its huge rice exports, Koreans were able to retain little of the crops for their own consumption. (**Below**) Like much of the peninsula's heavy industry, the Japanese-built Korekawa Iron Works was shut down after the surrender of Japan and remained idle for many months.

(**Opposite**) A Buddhist temple near Seoul. In much the same way that the Roman Catholic Church in Europe was responsible for education during the Middle Ages, Buddhist monastaries were the seat of culture and learning in Asia. Korean missionaries were sent to Japan in the sixth century to work among the barbarians and soon converted most of the islands' population to Buddhism. (**Above**) Farmers relaxing with a game very similar to European-style chess.

12

Some of the thousands of Koreans repatriated from Manchuria via Tientsin, China, pause on an Inch'on beach after removing their belongings from a US Navy vessel. (**Opposite**) A Korean youth delouses a refugee while cooks prepare a meal at one of the special receiving centers built to quarter the new arrivals. In addition to the roughly one million Koreans who drifted into the US occupation zone from northern Korea or were repatriated from Manchuria, another one and one-quarter million persons were returned to their homeland from Japan by early 1947.

A Joint Soviet-American Commission was formed to work out the details of Korean unification. Conferences began in January, 1946, were stalemated by 6 May of that year and adjourned. The Joint Commission reconvened one year later but the unification question had to be turned over to the United Nations when the negotiators were unable to reach an agreement. (**Above**) Lieutenant General John R. Hodge addressing the Joint Commission's first formal meeting, 16 January 1946. To his left is the head of the Soviet delegation, Colonel General Terenty F. Shtikov, and an interpreter. Shtikov had been the chief political officer (commisar) of the Soviet army group which invaded eastern Manchuria and Korea. Hodge commanded the 43d Infantry Division on New Georgia, the Americal Division at Bougainville and took command of the XXIV Corps in time to lead it at Leyte and Okinawa. (**Opposite**) US liaison officer Major C. J. Dougovito conversing with Alexander Sergeyevich Maslov of the Soviet delegation and a Russian supply officer, 16 May 1947. Maslov had also taken part in the previous year's talks.

A demonstration in Seoul during the run-up to the May 1948 elections. Police were called in when a disturbance broke out between Communist and nationalist factions. (**Below**) US personnel interrogate a young man suspected of trying to disrupt the elections in Kaesong.

Citizens of Kwangju arm themselves with improvised bamboo spears to protect their homes and vital installations from guerrilla attacks. (**Above**) Privates Oduel Fruge and Robert Shropshire man a .30-caliber machine gun on the 38th Parallel near Ch'ongch'on on the first free election day in Korea's history, Monday, 10 May 1948.

Refusing to be intimidated by Communist threats to burn polling places, volunteers stand guard as voters enter to cast their ballots in Cholla Namdo Province. (**Below**) An elderly gentleman and a woman with a baby strapped to her back vote in Pusan.

Election workers counting ballots in Kaesong.

Syngman Rhee (**left**) was made chairman of the newly elected National Assembly. Later that summer, the Assembly adopted a constitution and voted to make Rhee the Republic of Korea's first President. Above the Parallel, Kim Il Sung (**right**), a former major in the Soviet Army, headed a government formed by the Communist party.

After the withdrawal of the last US ground forces in June 1949, the Republic of Korea assumed complete control of its armed forces. Small arms, machine guns, jeeps, trucks and some light artillery were left behind and the US government promised to make available a six-month stockpile of maintenance supplies. It was not thought necessary to supply the Koreans with tanks, fighter aircraft and heavy artillery since their army was designed to be primarily an internal security force to protect the republic from insurgent forces within its own borders. (**Opposite**) A company of soldiers sing on the march and (**above**) a group of young officers, June 1949.

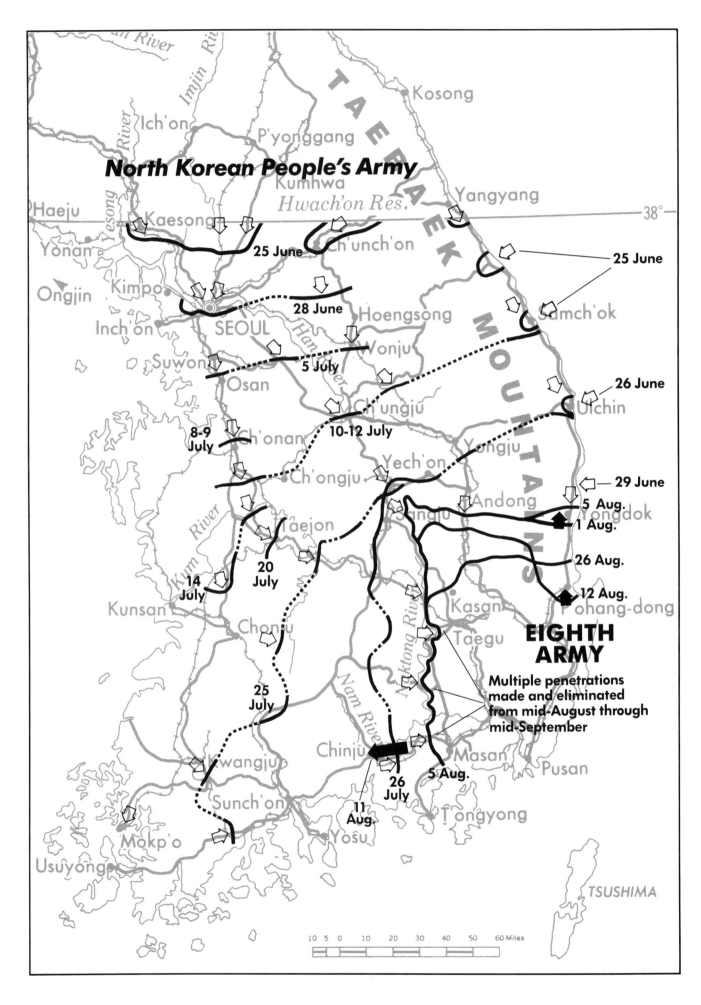

CHAPTER TWO

Invasion

The invasion of South Korea opened with a light bombardment of ROK positions in the Ongjin area at roughly 4:00 a.m. on 25 June 1950. It was a rainy Sunday morning at the start of the monsoon season and few ROK soldiers were at the frontier when the blow fell. Within an hour, heavy artillery fire was reported at locations all along the 38th Parallel and NKPA infantry, supported by 150 Soviet-made T-34 tanks, had crossed the border at several points. The North Koreans had achieved complete surprise.

The outnumbered and scantily equipped defenders quickly recovered from the shock of the initial assault but had no weapons to counter the NKPA's armored spearheads. The South Korean capital, Seoul, fell on the fourth day of the war and the premature demolition of bridges over the wide Han River forced the retreating ROK Army to abandon the little equipment it did possess.

Korean veterans of the Chinese Civil War and the prolonged struggle with Japan made up two of the NKPA's ten combat divisions. These divisions had been transferred relatively intact from the Chinese Army the previous year along with enough other battle-hardened Korean vets to make up the core of three more divisions. The eight-division Army of the Republic of Korea, on the other hand, was little more than an internal security force.

The Communists had planned to rapidly overrun the southern half of the peninsula before substantial aid could stiffen its defense. A quick victory would present the United Nations, which had worked hard to produce free elections, with a *fait accompli* by force of arms. The Communists, however, had underestimated the revulsion that such blatant aggression would generate. Upon hearing of the invasion, UN Secretary General Trygve Lie exclaimed: "My God! This is war against the United Nations."

The UN Security Council convened for an emergency meeting on 25 June and called on North Korea to withdraw its forces back behind the Parallel. When it became clear that the invasion was continuing unabated, a 27 June meeting recommended that ". . . the members of the United Nations furnish such assistance to the Republic of Korea as may be necessary to repel the armed attack and to restore international peace and security in the area." That same day, President Truman authorized General MacArthur in Tokyo to provide the South Koreans with air and naval support.

Curiously, the ROK owed at least some thanks to the Soviet Union for the massive, world-wide support it was about to receive. That the UN was able to act so quickly and decisively, instead of getting bogged down in endless debates, was due to the fact that the Soviet delegate to the Security Council was not present to veto its resolutions. The Soviets had been boycotting the Security Council's meetings for five months because of its refusal to give Nationalist China's seat to the Red Chinese in Beijing.

By the end of June it was readily apparent that the ROK did not have the means to stop the Communist juggernaut and that US combat troops would have to be introduced. The United States had four understrength (and somewhat flabby) divisions on occupation duty in Japan and from these slender resources would have to come the troops to repel the invaders.

Elements of the 24th Infantry Division were hastily flown from Japan and thrown into the fight while the rest of the division followed by sea. In a series of bitter delaying actions between 5-20 July, the division traded 100 miles and nearly 4,000 men for enough time to allow the 1st Cavalry and 25th Infantry Divisions to join the remnants of the ROK Army in forming a defensive perimeter around the port of Pusan.

The initial contact between the 24th Infantry Division and the NKPA came when Task Force *Smith*, a battalion-sized formation, tried to block a column of infantry and armor moving south toward Osan. An attached battery of 105mm howitzers had only six rounds of antitank ammunition and there were too few soldiers available to protect the battalion's flanks from the North Korean infantry. Task Force *Smith* was driven back with heavy losses. Later, a fierce, two-day delaying action at Taejon cost the 24th many more casualties, including its commander, Major General William F. Dean, who had personally led a bazooka team on a successful tank-hunting expedition through the city's narrow, twisted streets. Dean was later captured and spent more than three years in a Communist prison camp.

Behind the thinly held Naktong River line, the Eighth Army, commanded by Lieutenant General Walton H. Walker, raced to build up its forces before the NKPA could mount a concentrated effort to seize Pusan. The 2d Infantry Division, 1st Provisional Marine Brigade and two regimental combat teams were funneled through the port to critical spots on the line as was the British 27th Infantry Brigade which arrived from Hong Kong on 29 August. During this period, UN airpower grew rapidly and the North Koreans were relentlessly hammered by strikes launched from aircraft carriers and bases in Japan.

Although reinforcements poured into the Pusan perimeter, the Eighth Army still lacked enough troops to form a defense in depth. Instead, large mobile reserves, were gathered together and shifted from one threatened sector to another. The front line— little more than strong points strung out along the hill tops and valley roads—was repeatedly broken by determined assaults and infiltrations launched at night in an effort to minimize the effectiveness of UN airpower. General Walker's use of short, quick counterattacks against the penetrations prevented the NKPA from maintaining the initiative. UN forces succeeded in defending the key cities of Masan, in the south, and Taegu, in the center, while P'ohang-dong, on the east coast, changed hands several times.

Intense Communist attacks continued almost without letup into the middle of September. The North Koreans, however, were clearly reaching the end of their rope. They had expended most of their tanks in earlier fights, and now their troops were literally beginning to starve, as US, British and Australian flyers continued to wreak havoc on their supply lines. The veterans of the Chinese Army had, by now, almost all been killed on battlefields from the 38th Parallel to the Naktong River and, in their place, were largely untrained recruits, many of whom had been dragooned from towns and villages in the South. Meanwhile, the Eighth Army's strength grew daily. Their own counterattacks were beginning to recover lost ground and the newly constituted X Corps in Japan readied itself for a blow far behind the Communists' lines at a place called Inch'on.

The easternmost of four bridges over the Han River near Seoul. The bridges were blown on the night of June 27-28 while three ROK divisions were still fighting north of the river. (**Below**) ROK infantry advance cautiously across a hillside, July 1950.

Lieutenant Colonel Lloyd H. Rockwell, advisor to the ROK II Corps confers with Brigadier General Paik Sun Yup at his ROK 1st Division headquarters. Paik was one of South Korea's finest combat officers and later commanded both the ROK I and II Corps. (**Below**) ROK recruits enroute to a battle area, 5 July 1950. These young soldiers carry antiquated bolt-action rifles but, like most Koreans, had excellent night vision, great physical endurance and learned terrain appreciation from a lifetime of walking instead of riding.

28

(**Left**) American dependents leave the Norwegian fertilizer ship SS *Reinholt* which made the trip from Inch'on to Fukuoka, Japan, with 682 women and children. (**Right**) Evacuees arriving at a Fifth Air Force Base, 27 June 1950. (**Opposite**) Buildings and a truck set afire during a strafing attack by F-80 jet fighters based in Japan. The knocked out T-34 tank and bomb craters at the bottom of the photo were from an earlier air strike.

The premature demolition of the Han bridges left the US Military Advisory Group cut off above the river. On the morning of Wednesday, 28 June 1950, they made the crossing on small boats east of the bridge pictured on the previous page. The Advisory Group was forced to leave their transportation behind but did manage to save the radio vehicle—their only means of communication with Japan— then marched 15 miles cross-country to Anyang-ni, where they were picked up by waiting trucks and brought to Suwon Airbase for evacuation. (**Below**) 24th Infantry Division troops of Task Force *Smith* arriving at Taejon's railroad station on Sunday, 2 July. Like the ROK, they also lacked adequate antitank protection and were badly mauled by North Korean armor three days later above Osan. (**Opposite top**) Eighth Army commander Lieutenant General Walton H. Walker (*left*) is greeted by Major General William F. Dean at an advance airfield near Taejon on Friday, 7 July. Walker arrived early in the morning with news that Dean's 24th Infantry Division would soon be joined by the rest of the Eighth Army. Dean was later captured after conducting an heroic defense at Taejon. (**Opposite bottom**) Walker discussing operations along the Kum River line with his staff on 14 July, the day after he established his headquarters in Taegu.

— A traffic jam of refugees, US and ROK troops at a Ch'onan street corner on 7 July, the day before the city fell to the Communists. (**Below**) Army engineers packing sandbags around high explosive charges on a bridge pier to maximize the force of the blast. As the NKPA continued to advance, bridge demolition became a major project of Army engineers.

An ROK crew prepares their 57-mm antitank gun for action in the Taebaek Mountains, 22 July 1950. (**Below**) ROK trucks being loaded with war supplies at a rain-soaked air strip, 2 July 1950.

An ROK soldier awaiting word to resume the march and (**opposite top**) exhausted ROK infantry stretch out during a lull in the fighting, 7 July 1950. (**Opposite bottom**) A South Korean crew firing their new 105-mm. howitzer in support of Paik Sun Yup's ROK 1st Division, 26 July. Paik, who in June led the division as a colonel and was now a major general, lost nearly half of his men in the opening days of the invasion. His division successfully withdrew across the Han River with their crew-served weapons but had no way to transport their vehicles and artillery. By late July, some of their equipment losses had been made up by a frantic US effort to resupply them from stocks in Japan.

A convoy of US and ROK troops speeds past refugees in central Korea. (**Right**) Private Jim Sullivan of the 24th Infantry Division watches for the enemy while his buddy gets a little rest. (**Opposite**) Front line troops receiving mail from home and flares lighting the sky over the Kum River Bridge. The bridge was destroyed in mid-July to keep it from falling into enemy hands.

(**Opposite**) 1st Cavalry Division troops board landing craft for their unopposed landing at P'ohang-dong on Tuesday, 18 July 1950. (**Below**) One week later outside Yongdong, a unit of the division observes enemy movements then returns fire from the area beyond the truck. The 1st Cavalry Division suffered 275 casualties on 25 July and was forced to withdraw from the town.

Reinforcements for Korea: (**Above**) Troops leaving the Seattle Port of Embarcation, 6 September, 1950. (**Below**) The British 27th Brigade arrived at Pusan from Hong Kong on 25 August and were quickly committed to the fighting along the Naktong River line. Within weeks, they had discarded their distinctive helmets for a variety of other soft headgear. (**Opposite top**) The 1st Provisional Marine Brigade, built around their 5th Regiment and 33d Air Group, landed at Pusan on the night of Wednesday, 2 August. Here they are shown being trucked to a threatened sector a month after their arrival. (**Opposite bottom**) 25th Infantry Division equipment being loaded aboard LSTs at Sasebo, Japan. The entire division was ashore by July 15 and launched the first large UN counterattack on Monday, 7 August.

An American captain speaking with a group of nuns at a train station within the Pusan perimeter, Thursday, 27 July 1950. (**Below**) Black soldiers of the 2d Infantry Division's 3d Battalion, 9th Infantry Regiment on their way to the front, Sunday, 12 August. Only months before the war, the US Army had begun to revamp its racial policies and combat attrition in all-white units forced a quick end to segregation. Sixty percent of all Eighth Army units were integrated by the summer of 1951 and battalions like the above were reconstituted along non-racial lines in October of that year.

1st Cavalry Division artillery firing outside Yongdong and (**below**) wounded soldiers at an aid station, Tuesday, 25 July 1950.

A tank commander directing his M24 Chaffee's fire and maneuver, Wednesday, 26 July 1950, and (**below**) a 25th Infantry Division Chaffee moving over rough ground near Hwanggan on the main Seoul-Pusan highway, 24 July.

Corporal Marvin Brown directing 1st Cavalry Division traffic on Patolio Bridge outside Taegu, Wednesday, 30 August 1950, and (**below**) a Marine message center during the fighting for Taedabok Pass on Wednesday, 9 August.

Men of the 2d Infantry Division's 9th Regiment getting hot chow on the Naktong River front, Sunday, 10 September 1950. Corporal Paul Abernathy serves (*left to right*) Corporals John Enersob, Emory Bainey and Harold Cartier. (**Below**) Soldiers receiving Holy Communion during Catholic services a half mile behind the front lines on Sunday, 30 July.

South Korean recruits marching to a training center in Pusan, Tuesday, 1 August 1950. (**Below**) Laborers building a sand bridge for tanks next to a lighter capacity pontoon bridge over a tributary of the Naktong River at Shunshu, Thursday, 24 August.

Pusan

In the first three months of the war, more than 100,000 men and nearly 2,000,000 tons of supplies and equipment arrived in Korea. The photo below shows a portion of Pusan's rail yard, Pier 2 (*center*), over which the bulk of US supplies were funneled, and Pier 1 (*left*). (**Right**) A boxcar is hauled to Pier 2 from the SS *Empire Victory* by a floating, 60-ton crane. (**Opposite**) Korean laborers sort through a jumble of supplies on the docks and load them onto boxcars.

Troops and barbed wire at Pusan Station. The vital rail line between Pusan and Taegu was never cut by NKPA forces during the Perimeter battles.

As US and ROK divisions withdrew towards Pusan in late July and early August of 1950, their support elements were forced to displace to the rear— or "bug out"— several times. (**Top**) L-5 light observation planes of the 25th Infantry Division's air section are parked along a road used as a taxiway on the central front near Sangju, Monday, 24 July, and (**botton**) the air section after its withdrawal to a field at Masan's harbor one week later. In the first photo, a group of Korean boys, who left their shoes behind at lower right, talk with Americans down the road.

Aircraft attrition was extremely high during this period, not so much from enemy fire as from the poor fields the observation craft had to operate from and from "engine burnout." Temporarily, at least, aircraft 418044 in the first photo didn't suffer the same fate as the unlucky plane in the background and was still operable a week later. It can be seen at center left in the photo from Masan.

NKPA forces would generally conduct a frontal assault against a US unit while sending one or more enveloping forces around the under-strength Americans' open flanks to establish ambush sites in the rear. In the opening days of the war, US units threatened with being cut off, invariably retreated and the whole process would be repeated at each successive defensive position. This situation persisted until enough divisions had arrived on the peninsula to form a weak but continuous line along the Naktong River and, by the latter part of August, extensive use of artillery and air power forced the North Koreans to increasingly limit themselves to night operations.

Another favorite tactic of the North Koreans was to disguise their troops as civilians and have them infiltrate US lines by mingling into the streams of innocent refugees moving south. Grenades would be thrown at passing Americans, a crowd stampeded or any other opportunity taken advantage of to add to the chaos along the roads. (**Below**) North Korean prisoners awaiting interrogation and (**right**) a partially camouflaged, Soviet-made GAZ-51 truck on a Han River ferry is abandoned in mid-river when a reconnaissance plane is apparently mistaken for an attack aircraft.

Two of four 24th Infantry Division soldiers captured and executed on the night of Sunday, 9 July 1950, as they were patrolling between a forward observation post and the front lines. The opening months of the war showed a tendency by both sides to take no prisoners and Americans who fell into Communist hands sometimes became the objects of hideous tortures or, more often, were simply shot. (**Below**) Sergeant Johnny R. Long of the 1st Cavalry Division keeps an eye out for the enemy while South Korean and American buddies grab some sleep on the night of Tuesday, 1 August. Although they were behind the front lines, one wonders what Sergeant Long thought of having a flash bulb possibly mark his position for patrolling Communists.

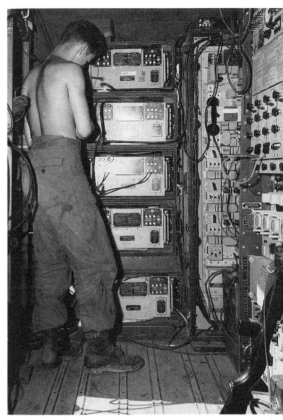

The extensive communications network employed by US forces helped alleviate their other deficiencies and allowed the Eighth Army to respond quickly to crisis situations. (**Opposite top**) A mobile radio unit coordinating artillery support, Monday, 10 July 1950. (**Opposite bottom**) Communications wires draped across the command post of the 25th Infantry Division's 27th Regimental Combat Team, Sunday, 20 August. (**Above**) The carrier terminal van of I Corps'advance command post being set up on Wednesday, 16 August. Note the carbine leaning againt the wall in the right hand photo. (**Right**) The Communist threat to Taegu necessitated that the Eighth Army headquarters, with its 4-van unit containing a 1,200-line switchboard and 180 teletype lines, be moved back to Pusan on 6 September to prevent its damage or capture. There was no equipment in the Far East to replace the communications unit and its loss would have greatly handicapped the Eighth Army's communications with Tokyo.

(**Below**) Soldiers fighting in a burning village, Tuesday, 15 August 1950.
(**Opposite top**) Marines observing their fire on a distant hill and (**opposite bottom**) an M26 Pershing of the 1st Marine Medium Tank Battalion supporting a leatherneck attack on Obong-ni Ridge, Thursday, 17 August.

A grief-stricken infantryman whose buddy has been killed in action is comforted by another soldier as a corpsman in the background methodically fills out casualty tags, Haktong-ni area, Monday, 28 August 1950. (**Below**) Marines holding a memorial service at a cemetary in the Pusan Perimeter in late August. (**Opposite top**) Marine Privates Valente U. Yruegas and Billy J. Lowrey at a bivouac area near Masan known as "the Bean Patch," Wednesday, 23 August. (**Opposite bottom**) 25th Infantry Division troops cross a damaged bridge northwest of Taegu near Waegwan, Tuesday, 29 August.

60

Refugees, carrying bundles of personal belongings, crowd onto an LST at Masan, Wednesday, 13 September 1950. Masan contained an extremely large number of Communist sympathisers and guerrilla attacks in the area occurred with disturbing regularity. At the height of desperate fighting a few miles to the west, the population was ordered out in an effort to facilitate the protection of the 25th Infantry Division's rear areas. On just 10 and 11 September, 12,000 people were removed by South Korean LSTs to a small island near Pusan.

(**Opposite top**) In an all-too familiar sight during the first year of the war, refugees stream south from Andong on the upper Naktong River, Saturday, 29 July. The understrength ROK 8th Division fought off the NKPA 12th Division's veterans of the Chinese wars for two weeks before being pushed out of the city on Tuesday, 1 August. (**Opposite bottom**) A village near Masan is burned to the ground to prevent refugees from returning to it and having guerrillas infiltrate them, Tuesday, 15 August.

The Naktong River meant nothing but misery to most Americans fighting for their lives in the Pusan Perimeter. But for this group of lucky Marines in the area where it curved eastward, away from the front, its waters supplied the pleasure of a much needed bath, Monday, 21 August 1950. (**Below**) Army privates Pete Escoto (*left*) and Lawrence Forlenza construct a barbed wire barricade, Thursday, 10 August. (**Opposite top**) US vehicles at a staging area south of Taegu, Sunday, 13 August. (**Opposite bottom**) Corporal James L. Lawson giving directions to soldiers at an information station at the Taegu railhead, Thursday, 24 August. The MP to his right is a South Korean.

Private Herman Freeze and a bespectacled Corporal James Hewitt of the 25th Infantry Division proudly display a North Korean flag captured west of Masan in the Sibidang-san area on Tuesday, 5 September 1950. (**Opposite top**) A newly-constructed pontoon bridge at Susan-ni on the Naktong River, Friday, 8 September. (**Opposite bottom**) Privates Robert Smith and Carl Fisher of the 25th Infantry Division fire on Communist troops from their ridgetop position 500 yards west of Haman, Monday, 4 September. Their battalion had recovered the position on Friday and killed nearly a thousand counterattacking North Koreans over the next two days.

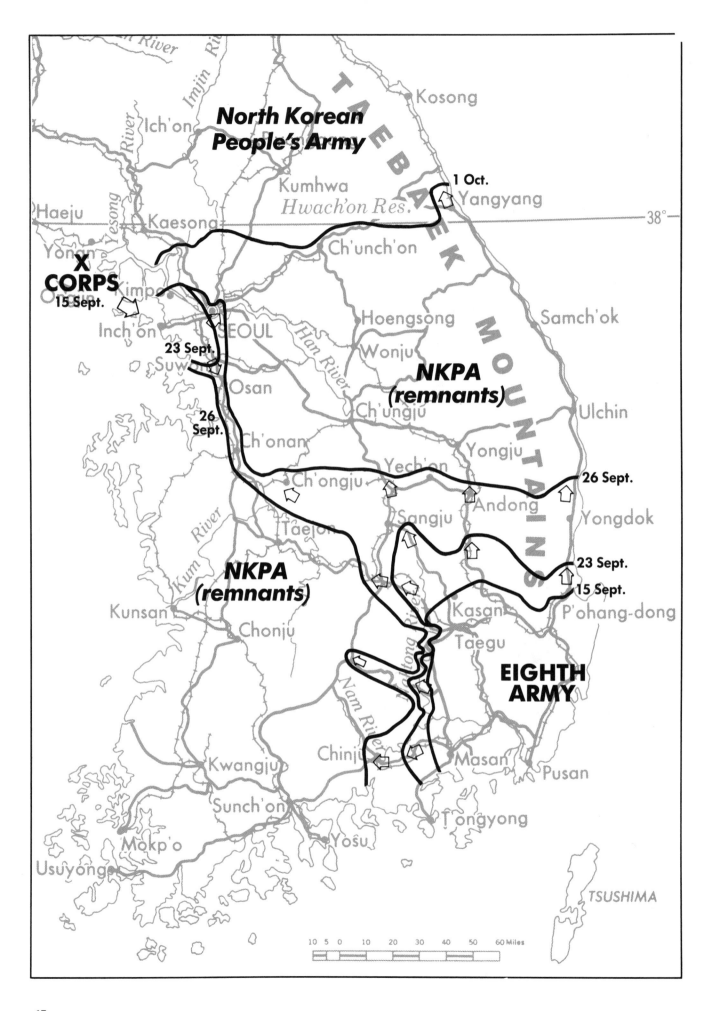

CHAPTER THREE

Inch'on
The UN Strikes Back

General MacArthur had considered using the 1st Cavalry Division to mount a seaborne assault on Seoul's port city of Inch'on in mid July, but the need for additional troops to stem the invasion was so overwhelming that the landing had to be called off. The meager amount of amphibious shipping collected was, instead, used to land the division unopposed at P'ohang-dong; within the shrinking perimeter around Pusan but away from the congested port.

As the fighting moved down the peninsula and away from NKPA supply dumps, the road and rail net emanating from Seoul became even more important to the sustainment of the North Korean offensive. These veins could be cut by a UN counterstroke at any of several west coast locations, such as Kunsan, Inch'on or the beaches near Osan. A landing at the northernmost site, Inch'on, entailed the greatest risks because of its dangerously narrow channel and extreme tides. What it offered, according to MacArthur, was the prospect of winning an important psychological victory through the quick, decisive recapture of the traditional Korean capital of Seoul. Moreover, it was such a bad landing site that it was only lightly defended and, with the bulk of the NKPA concentrated well away from the area, a UN invasion there was not likely to be endangered by strong counterattacks.

MacArthur's intention to invade at Inch'on generated such deep concern among the Joint Chiefs of Staff that two of its members, General Lawton J. Collins and Admiral Forrest P. Sherman, flew to his Tokyo headquarters on 23 July to, as Secretary of Defense Louis A. Johnson related, "try to argue General MacArthur out of it." Johnson, however, fully backed the Far East Commander's plan and President Truman backed his defense secretary. Less than a week before the 15 September landings, the JCS grudgingly approved Inch'on as the invasion site.

In spite of continued heavy Communist attacks on the Pusan Perimeter, MacArthur shifted nearly all Korea-bound reinforcements into the 7th Infantry Division of the newly activated X Corps in Japan. Like the other occupation divisions, the 7th was badly undermanned when hostilities broke out and was soon gutted to make replacements for the divisions already sent to Korea. In order to fill its depleted ranks, nearly 6,000 officers and enlisted men from the United States were assigned to the division in the weeks before the invasion. MacArthur's staff foresaw, however, that even though it was the sole recipient of the Korean replacement stream, the division would still not be up to strength by D-day. To make up the difference, half-trained Korean recruits were shipped to Japan to augment its units.

Roughly 100 recruits were attached to each rifle company and artillery battery, giving the 7th Infantry Division a total of 24,845 troops when it embarked for Inch'on. Called *Katusas* or *ROKs* (pronounced like "rocks"), the acronyms for Korean Augmentation to the United States Army and Republic of Korea, they had already been integrated into the US divisions defending Pusan, though not in the extreme numbers witnessed in the 7th.

Bombardment of the North Korean shore batteries protecting Inch'on's harbor began on Wednesday, 13 September, two days before the landings. Four British and American cruisers, supported by a half dozen destroyers and aircraft from the carriers of Task Force 77, eventually succeeded in silencing the heavily revetted guns on Wolmi Island, but not before the destroyers USS *Collett* and HMS *Gurke* were pummeled by nine and three hits respectively. The light cruiser HMS *Jamaca* also suffered casualties when strafed by two North Korean Yak fighters attacking the bombardment group.

The first assault landing since the Easter Sunday invasion of Okinawa, five years before, commensed at 6:33 a.m. on, Sunday, 15 September 1950 when a battalion of US Marines went ashore with the tide at Wolmi's Green Beach. The island was quickly wrestled from the surviving North Korean defenders and the Marines braced themselves for a counterattack as the tide rolled out leaving them cut off from reinforcements by impassable mud flats.

The balance of the 1st Marine Division's leathernecks came ashore with the evening tide. The division that assembled off Inch'on contained units from California, the Pusan Perimeter and the US Sixth Fleet in the Mediterranean as well as an attached ROK Marine regiment. Landing just south of the port and along Inch'on's seawall, the Marines found themselves hindered more by the blackness of night than the NKPA. They reached their final D-day objectives after midnight, and by the following evening had advanced far enough inland to prevent the North Koreans from shelling the unloading areas.

The first elements of the 7th Infantry Division were put ashore on D+3 as the Marines cleared enemy units from Kimpo Airport west of Seoul. Within hours, C-54 cargo planes were landing with ammunition and gasoline, then returning to Japan with wounded. Squadrons of Marine fighters were based at Kimpo almost immediately and provided much needed close air support to the soldiers and Marines fighting to expand their perimeter. The arrival of the 187th Airborne Regimental Combat Team at Kimpo on 24 September brought Major General Edward M. (Ned) Almond's X Corps up to nearly full strength for its drive to Seoul and the 38th Parallel.

The 1st Marine Division fought its way into Seoul's large industrial suburb of Yongdungp'o on Thursday, 21 September, and was soon joined by US Army and ROK regiments. Heavy, house-to-house fighting between UN troops and die-hard NKPA soldiers continued for seven days before resistance in the capital finally ended. By Sunday, 1 October, UN forces had chased the NKPA back across the 38th Parallel.

To the south, Communist units around the Pusan Perimeter stubbornly resisted an Eighth Army offensive timed to coincide with the Inch'on landings. US Army psychological warfare teams dropped hundreds of thousands of leaflets behind enemy lines to inform the North Koreans that Inch'on was captured, their supply lines were cut and that they would receive humane treatment as prisoners of war. At first, the NKPA held firm to its front line positions and few soldiers took advantage of the offer to surrender, but the number soon grew as the realization of defeat took hold. UN troops along the perimeter noticed the ring around Pusan start to disintegrate on 22 September as enemy units began pulling away to the west and north.

The retreat quickly degenerated into a rout. The bulk of the NKPA was bypassed and cut off behind US and ROK spearheads and, on the night of 26 September, a task force of the 1st Cavalry Division met 7th Infantry Division troops fighting their way out of Inchon. Ironically, the linkup occurred near Osan where Task Force Smith had made the US Army's first ill-fated attempt to block the invasion.

UN forces succeeded in capturing over 55,000 prisoners by 9 October but were unable to form a tight cordon across the peninsula. As many as 30,000 North Korean soldiers from six divisions seeped through UN lines while thousands more stayed behind in the South. In fact, so many turned to guerrilla warfare that the US 2d and 25th Infantry Divisions were forced to stay in southwestern Korea to deal with the problem. The NKPA was by now, however, a thoroughly beaten force, its best men dead, captured or in hiding. Above the Parallel, its remnants assembled in an area that would later be called the "Iron Triangle" where they reconstituted their depleted units and coordinated guerrilla activities in the liberated Republic.

(**Top**) Smoke from a two-day UN naval bombardment rises from Wolmi Island and the central harbor area beyond the jetty as Marines head south of the port to Blue Beach on the afternoon of Friday, 15 September 1950. Marines had landed on Wolmi's Green Beach on the morning high tide and quickly secured the island and its causeway to the mainland before the retreating waters isolated them from support. (**Bottom**) LVT3 amphibious tracked vehicles (amtracs) shuttle members of the 1st Marine Division between LSTs and an invasion beach. (**Opposite**) Marines assaulting Red Beach along the city's high, stone seawall used wooden ladders at the bows of their LCVP landing craft to speed their way over the top and move inland. They were followed by 22 more waves of leathernecks butting up against the seawall at clockwork intervals.

General of the Army Douglas MacArthur monitoring the invasion from the bridge of the command ship USS *Mt. McKinley* seems pleased with the operation's progress. Behind him are: (*left to right*) 7th Fleet Commander, Vice Admiral Arthur D. Struble; Acting Chief of Staff for Plans and Operations, Brigadier Edwin K. Wright; and X Corps Commander, Major General Edward M. Almond, 15 September 1950. (**Opposite top**) Leathernecks moving to forward positions pass three Soviet-built T34s knocked out by Marine M26 Pershing tanks near Ascom City on Saturday, 16 September. Hours earlier, F4U Corsairs from the USS *Sicily* knocked out two other tanks on the same road. Marine armor and bazookamen had just finished wrecking six more T34s the following day when a column of jeeps containing MacArthur, part of his staff and a gaggle of war correspondents sped into view and slammed to a halt among the carnage. After an appropriate amount of picture taking, the group roared off. Just after they left, seven fully armed NKPA soldiers were discovered in the culvert running under the spot where MacArthur's jeep had been parked. (**Opposite bottom**) Army engineers attempt to smoke out North Korean troops hiding in a cave near Inch'on, on D + 1.

The afternoon landing force coming ashore on Wolmi Island's Green Beach, Friday, 15 September 1950. (**Below**) LCMs carrying equipment and troops through locks protecting inner harbor docks from the extreme tides, Saturday, D + 1. (**Opposite top**) LCMs and a view of the inner harbor. (**Opposite bottom**) A group of LSTs on Red Beach continue to disgorge supplies while sitting high and dry on Inch'on's infamous mud flats. A fifth LST at upper right ran aground when it was unable to out-race the receding waters while still another above it safely negotiates the channel at low tide. Wolmi Island and the causeway connecting it to the mainland are at the upper left in this photo taken on D + 1 or later.

(**Opposite**) A small child cries in an Inch'on street and (**below**) residents fight fires which resulted from the previous day's street fighting, Saturday, 16 September 1950.

An offensive by forces within the Pusan Perimeter was planned for the day after the Inch'on landings but the continuous and intense combat along the front did not allow the Eighth Army to build up a large strike force for its breakout attempt. The troops were, moreover, exhausted after two months on the line and the trickle of replacements to infantry units had dried up weeks before when all troops from the States were directed to the 7th Infantry Division of the X Corps invasion force. Eighth Army gains were minor during the first few days of the offensive, as resolute North Korean defenders made frequent local counterattacks and clung tenaciously to every hill until decimated by concentrated firepower and determined, close-in assaults.

(**Opposite**) Troops of the 2d Infantry Division's 1st Battalion, 9th Infantry Regiment prepare to attack Hill 201 with the help of an M26 Pershing tank and M16 (quad-50) half-track mounting four .50-caliber machine guns, Sunday, 17 September 1950. Two days later, a platoon of the regiment's tank company succeeded in fighting its way to the very top of the hill and was instrumental in helping the infantry drive the enemy from the heights. On Thursday, 21 September, quad-50s came to the aid of the division when they and accompanying M19s armed with dual 40-mm. antiaircraft guns virtually swept NKPA soldiers from a two-and-a-half mile stretch of road near Sinban-ni. (**Above**) Brigadier General John S. Bradley, 2d Division Assistant Commander, and his staff observe the attack on Hill 201, Monday, 18 September.

Men of the 1st Cavalry Division's 5th Regimental Combat Team approach villages set afire by artillery rounds, Friday, 22 September 1950. The Combat Team had just captured an important hill mass south of Waegwan which dominated the Taegu Road. (**Opposite top**) Private Paul A. Rivers of the 2d Infantry Division searching for snipers in a burning village near Yongsan, Saturday, 16 September. (**Opposite bottom**) 7th Infantry Division troops and vehicles leave the transport USNT *General G. M. Randall* for Inch'on Harbor, Sunday, 17 September. The last of the 7th Division's combat units arrived one week later.

Platoons of the 24th Infantry Division's 19th Regiment take a break along a shallow depression near the Songju Road, Wednesday, 20 September 1950. Fighting had slowed considerably since the previous day's crossing of the Naktong River which cost the regiment roughly 50 casualties. (**Opposite top**) A fighter aircraft (*see arrow at upper left*) napalms NKPA mortar positions on the long finger ridge of Hill 174 which dominated a 21st Regiment's crossing sight six miles below Waegwan, Tuesday morning, 19 September. The regiment suffered 120 casualties during the crossing and, here, its men can be seen on both sides of the river with their assault boats. The ridge was taken shortly before noon and by Wednesday all three of the 24th Infantry Division's regiments and the attached British 27th Brigade were on the west side of the Naktong. (**Opposite bottom**) Casualties are evacuated back across the river on an amphibious jeep (often called a "seep" for seagoing jeep).

(**Opposite top**) A leatherneck searches for snipers near a destroyed Yak fighter at Kimpo Airport on the morning of Monday, 18 September 1950. The capture of Kimpo was one of X Corps' primary objectives and the three Corsair squadrons of Marine 33d Air Group were immediately based there to support the drive toward Seoul. (**Opposite bottom**) C-119 "Flying Boxcars" unloading special communications equipment and personnel, whose job was to get Kimpo back into operation, on Tuesday, 19 September. Around-the-clock operations were begun the following morning. (**Top**) 75-mm. howitzers on Marine LVT(A)4 amtraks firing in support of a 7th Infantry Division assault crossing of the Han River and (**bottom**) soldiers moving toward Seoul along the river's north bank after the crossing, Monday, 25 September.

A North Korean soldier captured by 7th Infantry Division troops south of Seoul is sent to the rear, Monday, 25 September 1950, and (**Opposite top**) Marines bringing back a group of NKPA prisoners after a sharp fight. At first, surprisingly few North Korean prisoners were taken in the Pusan area after they were cut off by the invasion at Inch'on. Few knew, in fact, that the landings had taken place and the UN Command took immediate steps to rectify that situation by dropping hundreds of thousands of leaflets stressing the futility of further resistance and promising humane treatment to those taken as prisoners of war. (**Opposite bottom**) A C-47 crew jettisons bundles of psychological warfare leaflets over enemy-held areas and an Australian soldier searching a North Korean for weapons. After an Australian battalion landed at Pusan on September 28 and joined the British 27th Infantry Brigade, the unit's name was changed to the 27th British Commonwealth Brigade.

(**Opposite**) Most NKPA troops fled north from Seoul through a hail of artillery fire and air strikes but die-hard units forced the US soldiers and Marines and an ROK regiment to battle for each block. Street fighting raged in the capital for three days before the city was declared secure on Wednesday, 27 September 1950.

(**Above**) General of the Army Douglas MacArthur leads the saying of the Lord's Prayer at a ceremony restoring the capital of the Korean Republic to its President, Syngman Rhee, on Friday, 29 September. Rhee and his wife, Francesca, are standing to MacArthur's left and US Ambassador to Korea, John J. Muccio, is to his right.

Armor and Tracked Vehicles in Korea

No large-scale armor battles took place in the Korean War and the tank versus tank actions that did occur rarely exceeded a half dozen combatants on each side. The North Korean invasion was spearheaded by approximately 150 Soviet-built T34/85 tanks organized into four regiments; three under first a brigade, then division, headquarters in the Seoul area, with the last attached to an infantry division in the east central mountains at Inji. The only US armored force immediately available to oppose them was a provisional tank battalion of fewer than 50 operable M24 Chaffee light tanks drawn from the four divisional reconnaissance companies in Japan. Seven M24s were lost to a combination of tank fire, close infantry action and artillery fire as they attempted to leapfrog to the rear during delaying actions above the Kum River on 10 and 11 July, 1950.

The thin-skinned M24s generally gave the thickly armored and heavily gunned T34s wide birth, concentrating instead on providing a mobile base of fire support for the infantry. Although a miscellany of other US tanks trickled in from ordnance depots in Japan, no significant reinforcements arrived until the second and third weeks of August when the equivalent of over seven medium tank battalions arrived in Pusan with nearly 500 M4A3 Shermans, M26 Pershings, M46 Pattons and Cromwell Mk IIIs.

The armor imbalance was now in the United Nation's favor and by November, tanks, aircraft and infantry armed with a more powerful bazooka eliminated 239 T34s. Forty of these tanks, as well as nine SU76 self-pro-

pelled guns, were destroyed near the Chinese border in the last flurry of fighting along North Korea's west coast road which included the war's largest— and last— tank battle. On Wednesday, 1 November, about a dozen M46 Pattons of the 6th Medium Tank Battalion engaged and destroyed eight T34s and one SU76 during a half-hour fight on the outskirts of Chonggo-dong, 18 miles from the Yalu River. One Patton had its muffler shot off and another was immobilized when a shell broke its track.

After the Eighth Army was driven from North Korea in December, NKPA tank forces were reconstituted and held in permanent reserve to guard the capital of P'yongyang. By April, 1952, the Chinese had also moved two armored and one mechanized divisions into the area to bring the total Communist armored strength to roughly 400 tanks and 150 self-propelled guns. None of this material was ever committed to battle against United Nations forces, but was the object of periodic air attacks which ostensibly destroyed more than a thousand tanks— or decoys— by war's end.

The Eighth Army frequently conducted armor-heavy reconnaissance in force missions during the first six months of 1951, with probes striking as far north as P'yonggang at the apex of the Iron Triangle. Thereafter, only an occasional raid, utilizing one or two platoons of tanks, would break the monotony of operations which inevitably called for tanks to act as little more than mobile pillboxes or direct-fire artillery.

M26

M46

The M24 Chaffee (**Opposite**) was a robust light tank which displayed a high degree of mechanical reliability. Unfortunately, its short recoil, 75-mm. M6 gun, which was adapted from the heavy aircraft cannon used in B-25H Mitchell bombers, could not penetrate the frontal or turret armor of the T34 even at relatively close ranges. The M4A3 armed with a high velocity 76-mm. gun, as well as many other improvements (**top**), was the most advanced variant of the Sherman tank produced during World War II. Although capable of engaging T34s on relatively equal terms, the gods of war gave them few opportunities to do so in Korea in spite of the fact that they were employed in large numbers. The Patton (**above**) was essentially the same vehicle as the Pershing but with a better gun, new engine and a cross drive transmission. Both tanks carried a big 90-mm. cannon and easily pounded into junk any T34s which crossed their paths. A quick way of distinguishing one from the other is to examine a vehicle's gun tube. Unlike the Pershing's tube which utilized a double-baffled muzzle break (*top*), the Patton's contained a bore evacuator, which helped minimize the escape of gasses back into the turret through the breech, below a single baffle. The M26A1 Pershing was armed with the same gun as the M46 but few, if any, appear to have been sent to Korea.

Captured Soviet-built armor at a salvage depot in Korea: (**top**) SU76 self-propelled 76-mm. guns, which the North Koreans often employed like tanks, and (**bottom**) T34 tanks mounting 85-mm. guns. (*Other views of T34/85 tanks can be seen on pages 74 and 103*).

Self-propelled antiaircraft weapons were used to devastating effect against Communist infantry throughout the war. (**Opposite top**) A fully-tracked M19 (dual-40) motor gun carriage armed with two 40-mm. guns. Half-tracked vehicles were also used extensively in this role. The arrival of even one M16 (quad-50) mounting four .50-caliber machine guns (*see page 79*) was a welcome sight to every UN unit in the neighborhood. Other self-propelled antiaircraft weaponry, utilizing several different combinations of .50-caliber or .50-caliber and 37-mm. guns on a variety of chassis, were employed against infantry but were much less common.

Cromwell Mk III tanks of the British 27th Infantry Brigade (*see page 144*) arrived from Hong Kong in time to take part in the drive to the Yalu and subsequent retreat to south central Korea. Cromwells had, together with the Sherman tank, made up the core of Great Britain's armored forces during the drive across northwest Europe in World War II. The Mk III variant, however, carried a gun which was considered inferior even by 1944 standards, the Mk 5 six-pounder, and the British quickly replaced their aging Cromwells with a tank that was arguably the finest fighting vehicle the world's armorers had yet produced, the Centurion (**opposite bottom**). The 50-ton behemoth protected its crew and 20-pounder gun behind six inches of steel plate and was more than a match for even the most modern Soviet-built tanks. Employed after the Communists decided discontinue use of their own tanks, it was limited to taking part in the same infantry support missions as the other less capable, yet adequate, tanks along the front.

94

The ability of US artillery to be either mounted on or hauled by fully tracked vehicles greatly added to its deployability in the rugged Korean landscape. (**Top**) The tube of a "Long Tom" recoils from the blast of its 155-mm. projectile. The gun is mounted on a modified M4A3 chassis and is operating in support of the 2d Infantry Division. Shorter-barrelled 155-mm. howitzers were mounted on a modified M24 light tank chassis and were commonly known as "Gorillas" (*see page 155*). (**Bottom**) An 18-ton M4 high-speed tractor, one of several prime movers which saw extensive use in Korea, is photographed pulling 7th Infantry Division heavy artillery ashore at Iwon, Sunday, 29 October 1951.

The "limited procurement" of M45 Pershing tanks armed with 105-mm. howitzers did not see action in World War II but were found to be particular-ly useful in Korea. (**Opposite top**) An M45 belonging to the 24th Infantry Division crossing a sand bridge across the Naktong River, Monday, 18 September 1950. (**Opposite center**) A Marine M4A3 dozer is seen after rolling off a pontoon barge on the north side of the Han River above Kimpo, Wednesday, 20 September. It carries the wide M1A1 blade and is armed with a 105-mm. howitzer. (**Opposite bottom**) US troops and Katusas of the 2d Infantry Division being ferried into battle aboard an M26 Pershing and M4A3 Sherman during an NKPA offensive aimed at Yongsan, Monday, 3 September. Like the 70th Medium Tank Battalion attached to the 1st Cavalry Division, the 2d's 72d Medium Tank Battalion apparently also contained a mix of Shermans and Pershings.

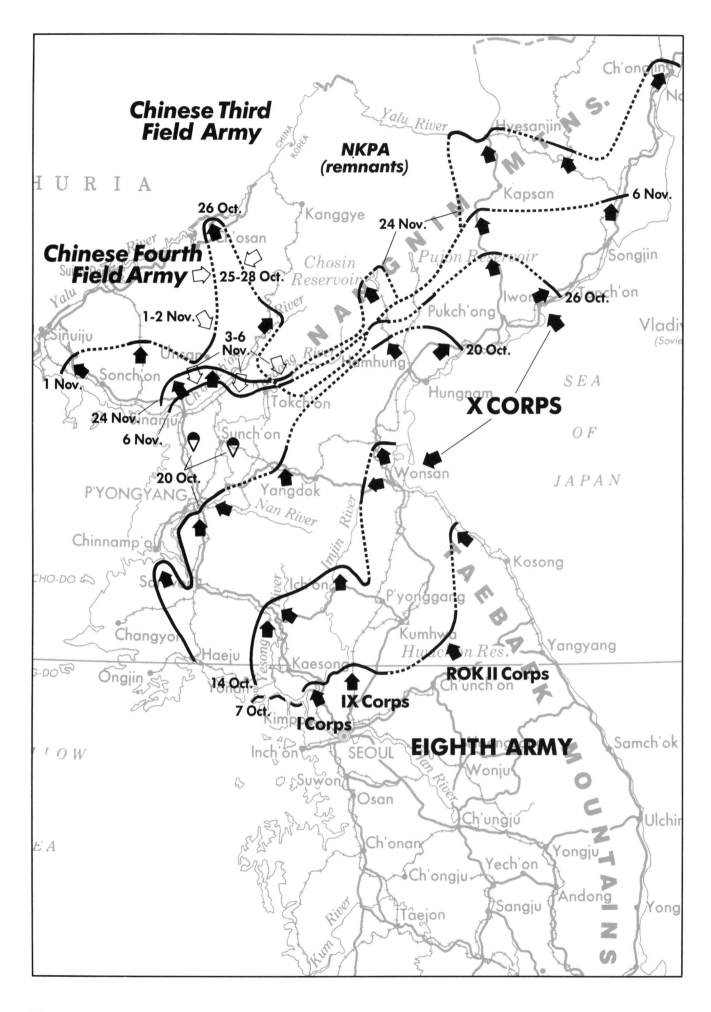

CHAPTER FOUR

Drive to the Yalu

Both MacArthur and the JCS believed that a restoration of the *status quo* along the 38th Parallel would not long curb the Communist's appetite and that another invasion of the South was inevitable if the NKPA was given time to reorganize. On 11 September, four days before the landings at Inch'on, President Truman approved a request by the JCS that MacArthur be allowed to plan for an assault across the Parallel if United Nations backing were obtained.

Not waiting for the UN's members to make up their minds, the South Korean government ordered their own troops north. Two divisions crossed the Parallel along the east coast on Sunday, 1 October 1950, with other divisions following in the mountainous interior. A week later, after much heated debate, the UN General Assembly voted to change the mission of its forces from simply repelling North Korean aggression to achieving a complete military victory and political unification of the peninsula. MacArthur was now free to attack the North.

The offensive began on Monday, 9 October, and by mid-month the NKPA's fortified positions above Seoul were overcome by the Eighth Army's I Corps made up of the US 1st Cavalry and 24th Infantry Divisions, the 1st ROK Division and the 27th British Brigade augmented by an Australian battalion. The North Korean capital of P'yongyang fell into UN hands after a light, two-day fight on Friday, 20 October and possession of its airfield helped alleviate the severe supply problems plaguing I Corps. The 187th Airborne Regimental Combat Team also parachuted north of the city on Friday to block retreating NKPA forces but met with only mixed success.

On the eastern side of the peninsula, the X Corps, which had reembarked with great difficulty from both Inch'on *and Pusan* over 200 miles to the south, arrived off the major North Korean port of Wonsan a day before P'yongyang was captured. Originally, MacArthur had intended X Corps to quickly land and slash its way inland toward the capital, thereby trapping most of the NKPA's remaining forces between it and the UN divisions moving up from the Parallel. The ground offensive, however, had far outpaced the amphibious movement and the approaches to the harbor were found to be exceptionally heavily mined. The Navy swept a channel through the thousands of Soviet-made mines and the 1st Marine Division was finally able to land on Wednesday, 25 October. They came ashore into the waiting arms of the ROK 3d Division and comedian Bob Hope's USO troupe.

The sudden collapse of the NKPA caught American military and political leaders by surprise and allowed little time for detailed policy making. The general line attained by UN forces in late October 1950 had originally been envisioned by Pentagon planners as being reached roughly a year later. JCS Chairman Omar N. Bradley firmly believed that amphibious landings, like Inch'on's, were a thing of the past and a methodical, broad-front advance— utilizing plenty of firepower to keep down UN casualties—had been projected by Pentagon planners.

The huge success at Inch'on surprised the Joint Chiefs and had, to all appearances, saved UN forces from a repeat of the brutal, drawn-out struggle up the mountainous Italian peninsula during World War II. Equipment and ammunition requisitions were cut back; reinforcements from other UN members, such as the Philippines, Canada, Thailand, France, the Netherlands and Greece, were thought to be arriving too late to see any real fighting; and many US soldiers thought that they would be back in Tokyo by Christmas.

During this period, the Red Chinese made several specific warnings against the use of US troops above the 38th Parallel. US leaders interpreted these statements as little more than a bluff to help stave off the defeat of their Communist neighbor and UN forces were allowed to move as far north as a restraining line running across the peninsula's narrow neck just above P'yongyang. The JCS believed that keeping UN troops well away from China's border would be enough to ensure that the Chinese Communist Forces (CCF) would not enter the war. Only South Korean soldiers would be allowed into the provinces along Chinese Manchuria.

At a 15 October meeting with President Truman on Wake Island, General MacArthur remarked that the Chinese would "face the greatest slaughter" it they intervened in Korea. This view was shared by the JCS and, shortly after his return to Tokyo, MacArthur moved the restraining line as close as 50 miles from the Yalu River separating Manchuria from North Korea. A week later, all restrictions on the maneuver of UN forces were lifted.

The Chinese Communists did not sit idle as UN troops neared Manchuria. Even as the Far East Commander and President Truman discussed the coming victory in Korea, the first of over 300,000 Chinese moved south across the Yalu. This force was composed of six three-division armies detached from the CCF *Fourth Field Army* and three four-division armies from the *Third Field Army*. Officially, these soldiers were "volunteers" serving under the NKPA commander in chief, Kim Il Sung, but it was actually China's foremost logistician, General Peng Teh-huai, who maintained control from the newly established joint CCF-NKPA headquarters in Mukden, roughly 125 miles above the Yalu.

Peng believed that he could adequately support his armies even in the face of the UN's massive air superiority. Marching almost exclusively at night and maintaining nearly flawless camouflage discipline during the day, the CCF massed in the hills to form several large traps ready to spring shut on any intruders moving toward the border.

The first hints of trouble came on Wednesday, 25 October, when Chinese prisoners were taken in the I Corps area. Then, in quick succession, CCF units violently attacked the ROK II Corps; forcing it to retreat nearly 15 miles; decimated a ROK regiment that had reached the Yalu at Chosan; and nearly destroyed a regiment of the 1st Cavalry Division which had been sent to restore the situation.

The Eighth Army's right flank was now dangerously exposed by the withdrawal of the ROK II Corps, while on the left, the understrength columns of its I Corps continued to plunge ahead. General Walker wisely recalled his far-flung spearheads and consolidated the Eighth Army along the Ch'ongch'on River on 31 October, while he assessed the situation and allowed critically needed supplies to catch up. Heavy fighting against the advance elements of the CCF continued for another week when, as suddenly as they had appeared, the Chinese infantry melted away to the north. UN Air reconnaissance failed to locate their major dispositions and no effort was made to keep the opposing forces in contact.

Across the rugged Nangnim Mountains, in the X Corps area, the CCF was unable to build up its strength as rapidly as it had in the west. A single Chinese division attempted to block the movement of the 1st Marine Division toward the Chosin Reservoir * and was quickly defeated, while the 7th Infantry Division, which reached the Yalu at Hyesanjin on 21 November, met only scattered resistance. Three weeks earlier, the 7th had disembarked at Iwon, 128 road miles north of Wonsan, arriving after the port's capture by the hard-driving ROK Capital Division. The Capital Division continued its assault up the coast road and, on 26 November, seized the large industrial center of Chongjin only 65 miles from the Soviet Union's Siberian border.

MacArthur was certain that the Chinese would not commit major elements of their army to Korea and their apparent withdrawal, after less than two weeks of fighting, seemed to confirm that they were primarily interested in protecting the important power plants supplying Manchuria with electricity from the North Korean side of the Yalu. The Communist's fear of the UN's overwhelming air superiority, MacArthur believed, would be enough to keep the Chinese at bay and their limited forces below the Yalu could be easily dealt with. The Far East Commander was, in fact, more concerned about the persistent guerrilla activities of by-passed NKPA soldiers, tying down the US IX and ROK III Corps in southwest Korea, than the Chinese Army.

On Friday, 24 November 1950, MacArthur's forces opened their final offensive to conquer what little remained of North Korea. They did not know that the Chinese Communists had already decided to commit themselves to war against the United Nations.

---

* Chosin was the Japanese name for the Changjin Reservoir. Although the US Army's official histories and the Korean's themselves use the name Changjin, the reservoir is most commonly know by the Japanese name made fameous by press reports of the day and subsequently used in the official US Marine Corps histories. All other Korean place names given in this book are in the romanized Korean adopted by the US Army as well as other government agencies and the National Geographic Society after World War II.

During the opening months of the war, the murder of US and ROK prisoners of war was a frequent occurrence generally believed to be perpetuated by frightened or vindictive soldiers in uncontrolled small units. But as NKPA troops attempted to extricate themselves from the south after the landings at Inch'on, mass executions of POWs, landowners, police, government workers and their families were carried out in a systematic manner. While it is difficult to estimate the number of people murdered in Seoul where the heavy fighting helped to mask atrocities, burial trenches filled with hundreds of bodies were found at Anui, Mokp'o, Sach'on, Kongju and Hamyang.

The bodies of approximately 500 ROK soldiers, hands tied behind their backs, were found near the Taejon airstrip. In Taejon itself, the city jail and Catholic Mission held 5,000 to 7,000 civilians, plus about 20 ROK and 40 US soldiers. Starting on September 23, they were taken out in groups of a hundred or more and led into shallow trenches where they were shot. Three civilians, one ROK soldier and two Americans survived long enough under a layer of loose soil to be rescued by 24th Infantry Division troops on Tuesday, 26 September 1950.

After crossing the 38th Parallel, UN forces discovered many groups of murdered POWs. Of the 370 Americans marched north from Seoul's Sodaemun Prison on 27 September, just before the city's liberation, about 300 were still alive on the night of Tuesday, 17 October, when they were herded into two freight trains in P'yongyang. The rest had died of starvation, dysentary or exposure. Many more died as the train creaked toward China and a lucky few slipped away to freedom. On Friday, as one of the trains took refuge in a tunnel from UN air strikes, the train's last 89 POWs were fired on while waiting for their evening meal in a nearby field. Twenty-one survived by feigning death or escaping into the brush. (**Above**) At a military hospital in Fukuoka, Japan, Bob Hope clowns with young soldiers who escaped from their guards and were safeguarded by North Korean civilians until the 1st Cavalry Division overran the area north of P'yongyang. They may be some of the POWs who got away from the train before the 20 October massacre. (**Opposite**) Murdered POWs discovered on Sunday, 15 October. The cigarette pack, discarded matches and crushed stubs seem to indicate that the men were held in this room for a while before being shot. A photograph of a wife or girlfriend lies at lower left.

102

(**Above**) A 24th infantry Division Sherman drives past the wreck of a T34 near Kumchon, the first large North Korean city to fall to UN forces, Friday, 6 October 1950. (**Right**) On their way to the Yalu River, Australian infantry of the 27th British Commonwealth Brigade climb make-shift ladders to cross a partially destroyed bridge at Pakch'on, Wednesday, 25 October. (**Below**, *left to right*) General Sir John Harding, Commander of British Land Forces in the Far East; Air Vice Marshal C. A. Bouchier, British liaison to MacArthur; and Brigadier Aubrey Coad, Commander of the Commonwealth Brigade northeast of Kaesong during the drive on P'yongyang, Friday, 13 October.

(**Below**) Troops of the 27th British Commonwealth Brigade's Middlesex Regiment continue their drive to the Chinese border as M4A3 Shermans of the US 89th Medium Tank Battalion fire in support, Friday, 27 October 1950. (**Above**) Middlesex radiomen relaying the positions of front line troops and NKPA dispositions. As the regiment moved closer to the Yalu River, resistance stiffened and they had to increasingly rely on air strikes and artillery preparations to help blast their way through.

NKPA soldiers marched to the rear by 1st Cavalry Division troopers, Monday, 23 October 1950. (**Below**) President Harry S. Truman takes General of the Army Douglas MacArthur by the arm and has a brief word with him before the two leaders depart from Wake Island on Sunday, 15 October. With them is MacArthur's aide-de-camp, Brigadier General Courtney Whit-ney. During their two-hour discussion of US policy in the Far East, MacArthur assured the President that any effort by the Chinese Communists to intervene in Korea could be easily countered by UN air power. (**Opposite**) A wounded soldier gets blood plasma while being sped to an aid center aboard a jeep.

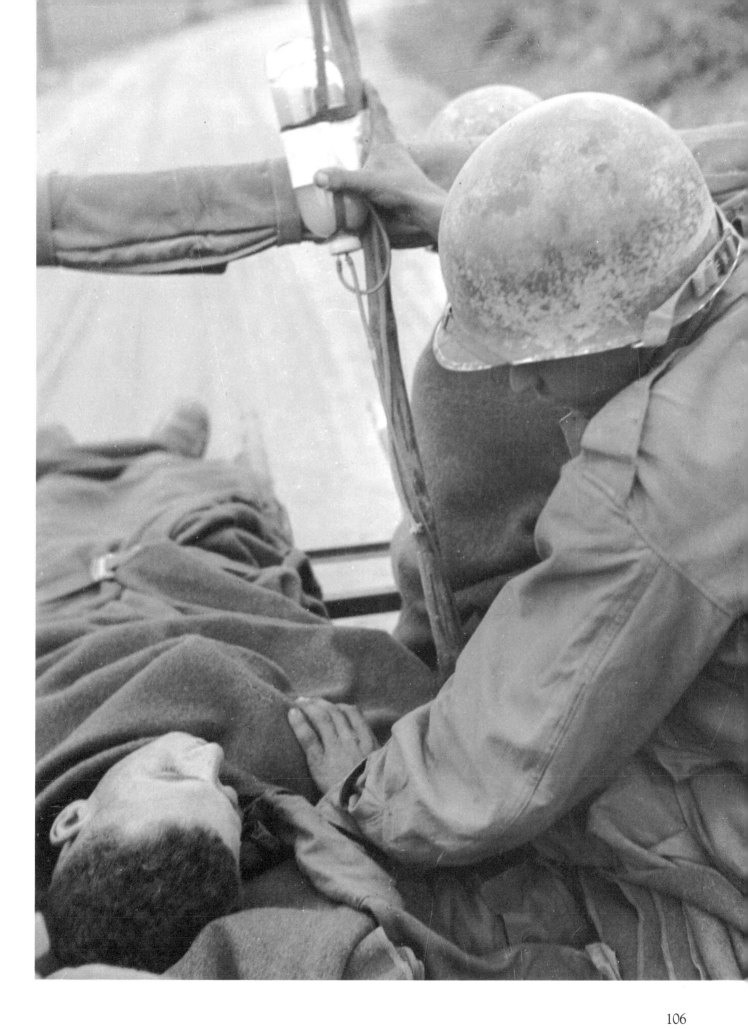

1st Cavalry Division troopers fighting their way through P'yongyang's rail yard, Thursday, 19 October 1950. (**Opposite**) Paratroopers of the 187th Airborne Regimental Combat Team wait in a light rain for orders to board C-119 transports at Kimpo Airport, Friday, 20 October. Heavy rains throughout the morning had forced them to delay their mission to block the NKPA's retreat routes through Sukch'on and Sunch'on, thirty miles north of P'yongyang. The assault had originally been scheduled for Saturday but had been moved up to dawn on Friday, because of the rapid pace of events. By the time the paratroopers began landing at 2 p.m., most of the targeted troops had already moved beyond the drop zones. (**Inset**) Paratroopers on the ground wait for one of the seven 105-mm. howitzers to come to earth. This was the first operation in which such heavy equipment was dropped directly into combat.

Sporadic rescue missions by Air Force and Marine helicopter pilots were taking place along the Pusan Perimeter as early as the first week of August, 1950. In late September the 5th Air Force sent a detachment of six Sikorsky H-5 helicopters to Taegu where they immediately proved to be worth their weight in gold. By the end of the war, thousands of injured UN troops had been evacuated by helicopter and many thousands more had their lives saved by helicopter lifts of food and ammunition to their embattled— and sometimes surrounded— positions.

(**Opposite top**) A Bell H-13 Sioux brings casualties to a medical collection point. The Navy and Marine designation for the Souix was HTL-4. (**Oppo-**site bottom) Sikorsky Chickasaws being guided into a landing site. The Chickasaw was designated the H-19 by the Army and Air Force and HRS-1 by the Navy and Marines. (**Top**) An Army Hiller H-23B Raven takes off on a spotting mission for the 2d Infantry Division. Its Navy version was designated the HTE-2. (**Bottom**) An Air Force Sikorsky H-5 evacuating 1st Cavalry Division wounded near Yongon-ni. The H-5 was the work horse for rescue operations during the first year of the war and was designated HO3S-1 by the Navy and Marines. Note the variety of casualty evacuation pods carried by these aircraft.

After a backbreaking logistical movement from Inch'on and Pusan that materially delayed the Eighth Army's drive on P'yongyang, the 1st Marine Division arrived off the key North Korean port of Wonsan to find that it was protected by thousands of underwater mines planted by the North Koreans under the direction of about 30 Soviet specialists. The Marines had to sail up and down the east coast for six days while a flotilla of 21 American, Japanese and South Korean mine sweepers suffered heavy losses clearing a channel to the beach. The landing was finally made on Thursday, 26 Octo- ber 1950. (**Opposite top**) Mine sweepers in Wonsan harbor as seen from the stern of the USS *Incredible*. The face of a grinning tiger shark is painted on one of the paravanes used for cutting mine moorings. (**Opposite bottom**) A South Korean mine sweeper explodes after making contact with a mine, Wednesday, 18 October. (**Above**) Landing craft heading for Blue and Yellow Beaches. (**Below**) Landing craft sit in the surf as a C-54 Globemaster comes in for a landing at an airfield captured two weeks earlier by the ROK Capital Division.

Severe supply problems plagued the drive to the Yalu and the Eighth Army came to increasingly depend on airlifts and parachute drops to keep its spearheads in motion. (**Above**) C-119 Flying Boxcars, their tail sections reaching to the sky like masts in a shipyard, are loaded with vital equipment and supplies at Kimpo while, (**below**) sitting atop the cockpit of his C-54 Globemaster, Major Alexander F. MacNiven turns his plane into a one-man control tower at Sinmak airfield between P'yongyang and the 38th Parallel,

October 1951. (**Opposite top**) Supplies being dropped to a unit near the front and (**opposite bottom**) Aircrew lashing supplies into place before take-off, November 1950. The "kicker" crew will later push the supplies out the cargo bay's massive rear doors. In the top photo, one skid of cargo (*see arrow*) drops like a stone past the other supplies when its parachute fails to open.

(**Below**) A well-camouflaged hangar, which used to house Soviet-built Yak fighters, is put to use by ground crews establishing an advance base for Marine fighter aircraft at Wonsan, Sunday, 29 October 1950. (**Opposite**) Leathernecks interrogating Chinese soldiers captured during the drive to the Chosin Reservoir. The Chinese troops who fought the Marines came from the temperate Shanghai region well to the south. Most were issued warm, quilted clothing and fur-lined hats but would suffer terribly in the coming December battles from a lack of gloves and low-cut, canvas shoes that offered no more protection from the snow and sub-zero cold than a pair of sneakers. Shortly before the 7th Marine Regiment smacked into Chinese units on Thursday, 2 November, their commander, Colonel Homer L. Litzenberg told his men that they might soon be taking part in the first battle of World War III. "We can expect to meet Chinese Communist troops," he said, "and it is important we win the first battle. The results of that action will reverberate around the world."

US troops and Katusas of the 7th Infantry Division move through the rubble-strewn streets of Hyesanjin near the Chinese border, Tuesday, 21 November 1950. (**Below**) X Corps Commander, Major General Edward M. Almond, *(center)* at Hyesanjin with 7th Infantry Division senior officers *(left to right)* Brigadier General Homer Kiefer, division artillery commander; Brigadier General Henry I. Hodes, assistant division commander; Major General David G. Barr, division commander; and Colonel Herbert B. Powell, 17th Infantry Regiment commander. (**Opposite**) US soldiers peer across the partially frozen Yalu River at a small Manchurian village. A bridge and temple in the valley below still burn from an earlier air strike.

Soldiers of the United Nations

Fifty-three of the United Nation's 59 member states voted their approval of the 27 June 1950 Security Council resolution calling for support to help the Republic of Korea resist aggression. Nineteen nations offered varying degrees of trade, technical or economic assistance, five sent medical teams and 15, apart from the United States, sent military forces. While their troops, whose numbers peaked at about 44,000, were often referred to by pundits and armchair generals as little more than a token force when compared to the US commitment of over 300,000 men, their forces fought courageously time and time again and boosted the morale of American soldiers.

Initial difficulties arising from language barriers, different standards of training and divergent tactical concepts, diverse dietary needs, religious and national customs all were reconciled. Most problems were easily solved but detailed planning was required for others. With the exception of the Commonwealth troops, who were eventually merged into a full combat division supplied out of British stocks, the other contingents were battalion or brigade sized units that were attached to American divisions after being reorganized, trained and equipped along US lines.

Different customs and tastes also presented unusual logistical and supply problems. All of the European contingents desired considerably more bread than US troops. The Dutch wanted their milk and cheese, and the French their bottle of wine. Because of religious restrictions, Turkish Moslems could not eat pork and Indian Hindus could not eat beef. The Turks, however, wanted strong coffee and butter instead of margarine while the Indians required rice and curry powder. Thailanders and Filipinos also needed rice as well as certain spices and strong tea. It was not too difficult a task to have American uniforms cut down in size to fit Oriental troops but acquiring shoes for diminutive Thai feet was a quartermaster's nightmare. The Turks and Greeks, on the other hand, had exceptionally wide feet.

(**Above**) A troopship arrives at Pusan with replacements for Dutch, Belgian, Greek, Ethiopian, Thai and Turkish units, June 1952. (**Opposite**) Colonel Boriboon Churajalitta inspects his Thai troops at the UN Reception center, November 1950, and Ethiopian officers talking with an American Sergeant, May 1951.

(**Above**) Fresh troops for the Greek Battalion arriving at Inch'on, January 1953; (**below**) battle-hardened Turkish soldiers near Imiang-ni, July 1952; (**opposite top**) French infantry using pack mules to transport supplies near Heartbreak Ridge, September 1951; and (**opposite bottom**) a Belgian machine gun crew keeping a close watch on nearby Communist positions, June 1951.

(**Opposite top**) A South African Air Force F-51 Mustang of the "Cheetah" Squadron taxis past fragmentation bombs and napalm canisters during a break in the weather at P'yongyang's East Airfield, late November 1950. (**Opposite bottom**) Mortarmen of the British 27th Infantry Brigade gas up their Universal Carrier before moving against NKPA positions west of Taegu, September 1950. (**Left**) A Canadian rifleman helps a wounded buddy to an aid station, spring 1951. (**Above**) A New Zealand artillery unit hauling supplies and 25-pound field guns to new positions, February 1951.

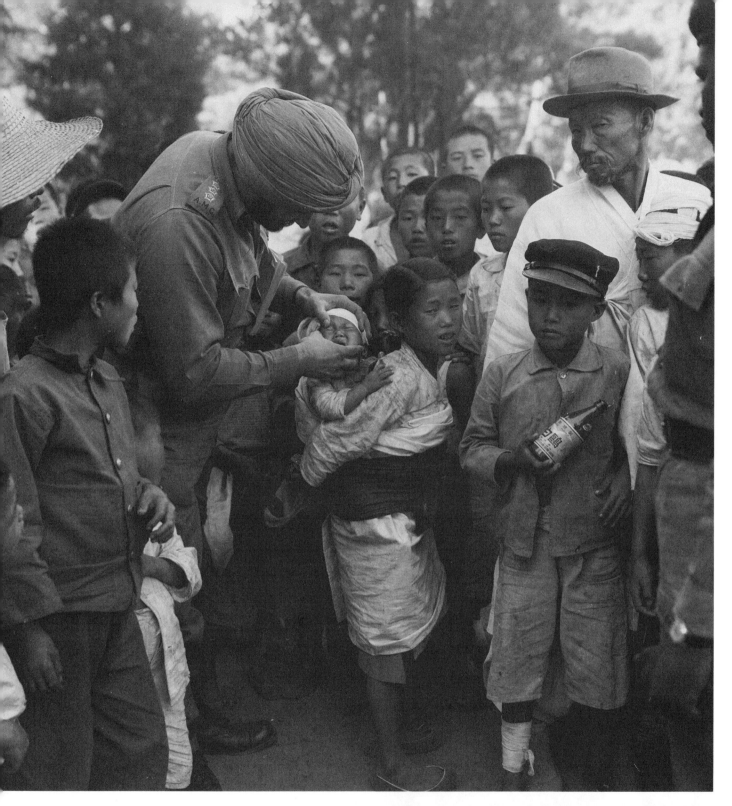

Indian medical officer Captain H. S. Parmar giving aid to Korean children near Taegu, October 1951; (**opposite top**) the surgical team of the Swedish Hospital in Pusan prepares for incoming wounded, October 1950; and (**opposite bottom**) Doctor Knude Kjrer watches as American and British soldiers match wits over a game of Monopoly on the the Danish hospital ship *Jutlandia*, May 1951.

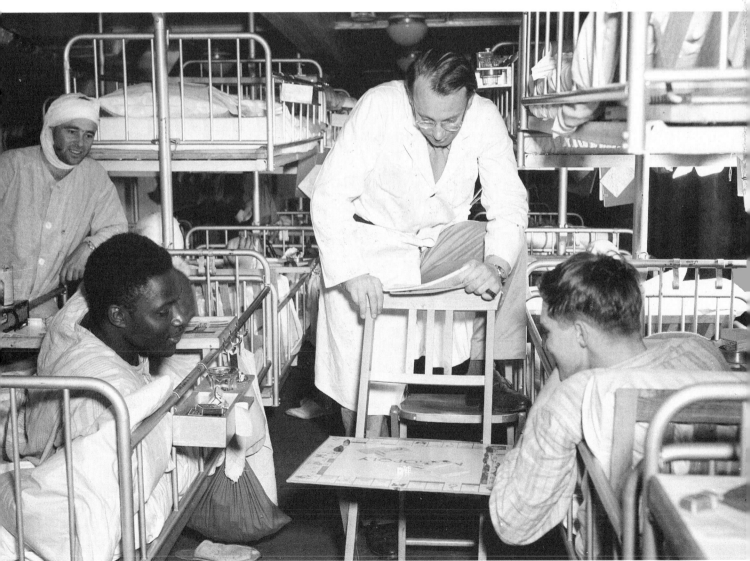

Chinese Third
Field Army

27–30 Nov.

Chinese
Fourth Field Army

25–30 Nov.

24 Nov.

5 Dec.

15 Dec.

X CORPS

5 Dec.

EIGHTH
ARMY

5 Dec.

1 Jan.

3 Jan.

10 Jan.

ROK I Corps

ROK III Corps

One NKPA division
infiltrated to this
area before being
scattered and
destroyed.

IX Corps

I Corps

X Corps

EIGHTH ARMY

CHAPTER FIVE

"An Entirely New War"

By Thanksgiving Day, 1950, the precarious supply situation had eased enough for most troops to enjoy a dinner of roast turkey with all the trimmings. There had been almost no fighting along the front since the CCF broke contact earlier that month and, with more than 140,000 NKPA soldiers in UN prisoner of war camps, hostilities seemed all but over. MacArthur, Walker and their generals were so confident of victory that virtually no orders were given to conduct aggressive, long-range patrolling to determine the location, size and intent of the Chinese Army.

The following morning, MacArthur's forces opened their final offensive. The Eighth Army, made up of the US I Corps, ROK II Corps and US IX Corps (now released from its counter-guerrilla mission), was to smash its way north from the Ch'ongch'on River bridgeheads while the X Corps, operating independently in the Chosin Reservoir area, attacked northwest to sever CCF supply lines. In subfreezing temperatures, UN troops moved forward against slight but growing resistance on all fronts; unaware that their movement had set off the tripwires that would bring China's phantom divisions down from their mountain fastness'.

Early on the morning of Saturday, October 25, the CCF struck. Accompanied by the distant, scratchy peal of tinny bugles and the staccato of exploding mortar rounds, a human wave of Chinese infantry smashed into and destroyed the forward units of the ROK II Corps. This corps made up the Eighth Army's right flank and General Walker was

forced to commit nearly all his reserves to keep his divisions from being encircled. Both the 1st Cavalry Division and the newly arrived Turkish Brigade were thrown into the fight and repulsed with heavy losses. On 27 November, UN forces began a costly withdrawal across the Ch'ongch'on. In covering this retreat, the IX Corps' 2d Infantry Division suffered roughly 5,000 casualties and lost most of its artillery as it fought its way to the river and then through a mountain pass south of Kunu-ri.

The Eighth Army abandoned the North Korean capital of P'yongyang on Tuesday, 5 December, after detroying mountains of carefully stockpiled supplies to keep them from falling into Communist hands. The US 25th and ROK 1st divisions as well as the British 27th and newly-arrived 29th brigades withdrew across the Ch'ongch'on as a fleet of two Australian, one American and three Canadian destroyers escorted shipping out of the river's estuary. Several hundred thousand North Koreans also fled before the invading Chinese and caused major disruptions to the army's movement south.

Across the peninsula, General Almond's X Corps was also struck. Three battalions of the 7th Infantry Division were overrun east of the Chosin Reservoir and the 1st Marine Division, strung out along 78 miles of a single, frozen mountain road, found itself isolated by three CCF divisions. The corps' four widely-scattered US Army and ROK divisions were immediately pulled back to defend the ports of Wonsan and Hungnam, while the Marines formed perimeters around their Kot'o-ri, Hagaru and Yudam supply bases. At his headquarters in Hagaru, the Marines' commander, Major General Oliver P. Smith, was asked by a war correspondent if his troops were going to retreat to the coast. Smith replied that since his men were surrounded—now by elements of six Communist divisions— there was no rear to retreat to and later added that the Marines were simply, "attacking in another direction."

Throughout the 13-day running fight, the quality of the close air support provided by Navy, Marine and Air Force pilots was astounding; and when the Chinese destroyed the only bridge that would allow vehicles to cross a deep gorge near Koto-ri, even bridging material was airdropped so that the Marines could continue their southward "advance." They linked up with the 3d Infantry Division on Sunday, 10 December, and were soon evacuated. The perimeter around Hungnam contracted steadily as more units were pulled out and, on Christmas Eve, the last of X Corps' 105,000 soldiers boarded a UN fleet of 193 ships. They took with them over 91,000 refugees, 350,000 tons of supplies and, unlike the Eighth Army which lost much of its heavy equipment, over 17,500 vehicles. Another 3,600 wounded or frostbitten troops and 200 vehicles had also been airlifted out.

Within days of the Chinese onslaught, it was obvious that they were in Korea not to form a buffer along their border but, instead, to annihilate the UN army. MacArthur reported that his men were up against an "overwhelming force" and that "consequently, we face an entirely new war." General Peng had apparently planned to envelop the separate UN forces and drive them into pockets on the coasts where they could be destroyed at will. But while the CCF displayed great tactical mobility by continually marching through the hills to form ambushes behind the road-bound UN columns, abundant motor transport in the west and control of the sea in the east facilitated the withdrawals.

By Christmas, the Eighth Army had generally reached the 38th Parallel but was not sufficiently organized to resist the attacking Communists. Seoul changed hands for the third time in six months and when CCF troops flooded through a gap on the 2d Infantry Division's right, the division was able to extricate itself from Wonju only after seri-

ous fighting and the timely commitment of the 3d and 7th Infantry Divisions. In mid-January, the Communists were finally slowed to a halt just south of Osan by lack of supplies and murderously heavy casualties while, on the eastern flank, the 1st Marine Division repulsed a deep NKPA infiltration which threatened ROK supply routes.

During this period, MacArthur pressed vigorously for an expansion of the war into China, arguing that it was virtually impossible to win against an army operating from behind an inviolate frontier. He predicted that if the Communists could not be attacked in their "sanctuaries," UN forces would face a "savage slaughter" and that "unless some positive and immediate action is taken. . . steady attrition leading to final destruction can reasonably be contemplated."

But while the Communists operated from the sanctuary of Manchuria, so, too, did the UN out of Japan. The JCS believed that if the war spilled beyond Korea's shores, the US would be hard-pressed to defend the island nation against combined Chinese-Soviet air attacks and keep it supplied in the face of a determined blockade by the 100-strong Soviet submarine fleet based in nearby Vladivostok. MacArthur's useless assurances that the Soviet Union would stay out of a general war between the United Nations and Red China were ignored.

Both the JCS and the British Government counseled against the US being sucked deeper into a widening conflict in the Far East. In 1950, no one knew if Korea represented the opening shots in a new world war and perhaps the aim of the Chinese Communists was to tie down US forces in Asia while the Soviets struck in Europe.

President Truman decided to abandon the objective of unifying the Korean peninsula and the UN consented to a resumption of its original aim— preserving the Republic of Korea. In mid-January, JCS members, J. Lawton Collins and Hoyt S. Vandenberg, flew to Tokyo and handed MacArthur a personal letter from the President in which he outlined "our basic national and international purposes" in Korea. General Collins also wanted to take a firsthand look at the situation on the ground and see how the Eighth Army was faring, now that it was under the command of his former Deputy Chief of Staff, Lieutenant General Matthew B. Ridgway.

Bob Hope and Marilyn Maxwell entertaining an infantry division in late October 1950. The show was done so close to the front that the troops still had their personal weapons with them. (**Right**) Air Force personnel at one of Mr. Hope's performances near Seoul. During his show at the "Wonsan Paladium" on Tuesday evening, October 24, Marine pilots and air maintenance crews— who had inadvertently beaten the Marine assault force to the city— were delighted to hear him crack jokes about their brethren sailing back and forth outside the harbor in "Operation Yo-Yo."

A wide variety of entertainers went to Korea during the hostilities to cheer up the troops. (**Opposite bottom**) Yodler Elton Britt of the Camel Caravan variety show performing for the 7th Infantry Division at Hongch'on and (**opposite top**) Marilyn Monroe with a star-struck airman at Brady Field in southern Japan. Marilyn appears to have sprained her right thumb, but it is likely that there was no shortage of medical personnel willing to assist her.

A Canadian truck convoy winds its way along a precarious mountain road. Narrow, badly drained and poorly surfaced, Korean roads remained inadequate to the needs of the Eighth Army throughout the war in spite of the herculean efforts of military engineers. Often the only "road" through an area was nothing more than an ox-cart trail which had to be bulldozed to make it wide enough for the passage of a single line of jeeps and "deuce'n'-a-half" ton trucks, then widened yet again to accommodate tanks and prime movers. Snow and ice made the roads treacherous in the winter and the monsoons created wide-spread flooding and rockslides in the summer. The nature of the terrain ensured that road traffic would be highly vulnerable to guerrilla attacks. In some parts of the country, convoys were regularly fired upon and even ambushed during the first year of the war as were other convenient targets such as signals relay stations on isolated hilltops and rail lines.

(**Opposite top**) A pre-World War II photo of the highway bridge spanning the Yalu River between An-tung, China, and Sinuiju, Korea. By the time hostilities erupted in 1950, a parallel, double-track railroad bridge had been constructed over the spot where the photograph had been taken. Both bridges were the focus of repeated raids by B-29 bombers and carrier-based aircraft between 8-21 November 1950. While spans were knocked down on this and other important bridges at Manp'ojin and Chongsongjin on 25 and 26 November respectively, the railroad bridge and another at Namsan-ni were never destroyed. In any event, attacking the Yalu bridges turned out to be like locking the barn door after the horses had bolted, since approximately 300,000 Chinese troops had already flowed across them from Manchuria by the third week of November and the sub-zero temperatures of December allowed even vehicles to cross the Yalu's frozen surface. (**Opposite bottom**) The Korean highlands above Kanggye looking across the Yalu into Manchuria west of Manp'ojin. Before being attacked by the Chinese near the Chosin Reservoir, the 1st Marine Division had been ordered to cut the Communist's supply route through this area. (**Above**) Lab technicians of the 548th Reconnaissance Technical Squadron processing thousands of aerial photographs during a graveyard shift. The quality of Chinese camouflage discipline was so high that overworked photo interpreters and other US intelligence assets located less than a third of the massive strike force gathering to attack UN forces.

China Strikes

The Chinese "volunters" who fell into UN hands in mid-October 1950 talked freely about the build-up of enemy forces across the UN front. US intelligence, however, was reluctant to accept their statements as reliable indications of a Chinese Communist decision to intervene in a conflict that was widely-believed to be almost over. (**Opposite**) Propaganda photographs of "fearless People's Volunteers marching to crush the imperialist Yankee aggressors and their running-dog lackeys."

(**Above**) Soldiers of the CCF *Fourth Field Army* during the waning days of the Chinese Civil War. Major elements of this army were later sent to Korea. Unlike the NKPA, which was a relatively heavy combat organization built along Soviet lines and armed with an abundance of Soviet equipment, the CCF was a light force whose soldiers were well trained in infiltration tactics. It was a tough, seasoned force armed with a conglomeration of Japanese, British, Soviet and American arms captured or supplied to them during the previous decades of constant fighting. The soldier in the foreground is armed with an American-made .45-caliber Thompson sub-machinegun, a weapon that the Chinese Communists had accumulated in such large quanties that they manufactured special slotted aprons for holding large numbers of bullet clips for their Tommy gunners.

(**Top**) A unit commander briefing subordinates at a forward observation post. Note the variety of clothing. The uniform colors of the troops fighting the X Corps in the the east were generally olive, white or khaki while those fighting the Eighth Army in the west wore the same colors plus a yellowish tan, dark olive and grey. Troops in the X Corps area came from east central China and wore quilted uniforms but were not issued boots or gloves. Across the peninsula, the troops, which were largely drawn from Manchuria, had fewer quilted uniforms but much better foot and hand protection.

(**Center** and **bottom**) Chinese pack artillery being hauled up a hill and a mortar position in action. No heavy artillery was used by the Chinese in their two 1950 offensives. Each division contained a pack artillery battalion with about 150 horses, mules or donkeys lugging a wide assortment of foreign-made light howitzers, recoilless rifles, heavy mortars and all the ammunition they could fit into 30-50 small carts. Air attacks on these units inevitably led to the logging of some rather odd entries into operational reports such as "attacked and destroyed military caravan: 17 wagons, 31 ponies and 16 camels." The battalions were also very careful about expending the limited amount of ordnance they carried. They had to be since there was no way they could be quickly resupplied. Once an ammunition cart ran out of shells, it could stay empty for weeks.

Huge quantities of American-made weapons fell into Communist hands as a result of the defeat of Generalissimo Chiang Kai-shek's Nationalist armies in the Chinese Civil War. (**Opposite top**) Water-cooled .30-caliber Browning machineguns. About an arms length of belted cartridges has been pulled from the first weapons ammunition box to give the propaganda photograph a more exciting look. (**Opposite bottom**) Chinese troops with trucks and 105-mm. guns of the 1st Cavalry Division or ROK II Corps in the Unsan area. This photo was probably staged at a later time since all, or most of the lost artillery was overrun between 27 October and 2 November 1950 in actions that occurred in early morning darkness.

Throughout the early fighting, the main weapon the Chinese used to counter US tanks was the satchel charge. Containing five pounds of TNT, the blast from one charge was usually enough to immobilize a tank by breaking its track. The attacking soldier, however, had to be able to get himself close enough to the vehicle to actually place the charge on the track for any damage to be done, and friendly tank or infantry fire usually stopped these suicide rushes. As for battlefield communications, use of radios and field telephones was virtually nonexistant below division headquarters in 1950-51 and units of all sizes commonly kept in touch through runners. Bugles were used to signal tactical maneuvers at the battalion level while whistles served the same purpose for company commanders and, perhaps, platoon leaders.

Elements of the Turkish Brigade which was badly mauled east of Kunu-ri on 28-29 November 1950. (**Below**) Australian troops of the 27th British Commonwealth Brigade crossing a pontoon bridge over the Taedong River near P'yongyang during the UN retreat from North Korea. US Army engineers are reinforcing the bridge with lumber. (**Opposite**) Engineers preparing to destroy a railroad bridge outside P'yongyang place satchel charges on its supports, Friday, 1 December.

(**Opposite top**) A rocket-armed F-51 Mustang piloted by Captain G. B. Lipawsky of the South African Air Force begins another mission against the Chinese from Suwon Airfield, south of Seoul, on Sunday, 17 December 1950. US and South African Mustangs had just completed their move from Pusan to P'yongyang's East Airfield on 22 November when the Chinese offensive forced their displacement to Chinhae, an old Japanese airfield near Pusan, after only ten days in the north. Operations from Chinhae were staged through Suwon until 5 January when the field had to be abandoned to the advancing Communists. During these moves, not a single day of air strikes was lost in spite of the fact that much equipment had to be left behind and destroyed in P'yongyang. (**Opposite bottom**) Members of an Air Force communications detachment receiving Holy Communion from Chaplain Martin W. Baumgaertner in a shell-scarred room, Tuesday, 28 November. (**Above**) Cromwell Mk III tanks of the British Commonwealth Brigade entering Seoul as the Eighth Army set up a defense line running generally along the 38th Parallel, Wednesday, 27 December.

On the night of Monday, 27 November 1950, two days after the CCF opened their second offensive against the Eighth Army in the west, well-coordinated attacks on the X Corps' left flank carved the 1st Marine Division and a regimental combat team from the 7th Infantry Division into what the Chinese hoped would be five easily digestable pieces. The 7th lost over 4,500 US soldiers and Katusas when its RCT was swallowed almost whole on the east side of the Chosin Reservoir at Sinhung-ni, but the Marines on the west side managed to consolidate at Yudam-ni, then fight their way down a treacherous mountain road to the next isolated Marine position at Hagaru between 1-4 December.

(**Above**) A forward air controller watches anxiously for the arrival of fighter aircraft while the Marine at right cranks an electric generator to power the radio. The continuous close air support supplied to the 1st Marine Division by Navy and Marine pilots was a key element in its successful movement from the Chosin Reservoir to Hungnam on the Sea of Japan. (**Opposite**) Traces of white from earlier snowfalls dotted the area when the fighting began but, starting on the night of 28-29 November, a series of severe storms blowing out of Manchuria added to the misery of Americans and Chinese alike. At night, when the fighting was often at its heaviest, temperatures dipped as low as 30-degrees below zero and some Chinese prisoners were brought in with their gloveless hands frozen to their weapons.

(**Opposite**) Critically needed supplies are dropped at Hagaru. The collection of tightly packed buildings and tents at the photo's center is the headquarters of the 1st Marine Division. This photo was probably taken on Tuesday, 28 November 1950, and the Air Force cameraman's shutter froze shut immediately after he took the shot. After a slow start, the Combat Cargo Command's airdrop machine was running up to 250 tons of supplies a day to Yudam-ni, Hagaru, Sinhung-ni and Kot'o-ri. A portion of the supplies were landed by Air Force, Marine and Greek Air Force C-47 cargo planes on small strips hacked out of the frozen earth at Hagaru and Kot'o-ri. Of even greater importance, the planes flew out 4,689 wounded or frost-bitten troops. (**Above**) A contingent of Marines awaiting word to move out toward Hungnam is starkly visible against a blanket of snow.

F4U Corsairs bombing the lower slopes of Hagaru's East Hill during the breakout to Kot'o-ri, Monday, 6 November 1950. (**Above**) After dropping its napalm canister behind a group of tents along the road and narrow gauge railroad tracks, a Corsair pulls up through the smoke from a previous blast. Directly beneath the Corsair, a weakened Marine is supported by two buddies. The tents had been abandoned by Army engineers when the Chinese attacked on the night of 28 November. Although they were located in a no man's land under the guns of a Marine weapons company, the company's commander related that "the abandoned camp drew the Chinese from the East Hill like a magnet because of all the goodies it contained." (**Opposite top**) An M2 light bulldozer is parked in front of the Marines and two M26 Pershing tanks are flanking a group of vehicles and crated supplies beside the tracks. One is near the tents and the other is visible between the gun barrel and helmet of the Marine at the right of the photo. This area was a sore spot in the Marines' defense throughout the CCF seige of Hagaru and is located to the southeast of the ground pictured on page *147*. During the breakout toward Kot'o-ri the bulldozer was sent forward to clear a Chinese roadblock and promptly knocked by three rounds from a captured US 3.5-inch rocket launcher.

A group of Marines guard the road as others in the background prepare to fight their way down the corkscrew corridor, Kot'o-ri, 9 or 10 December 1950. (**Opposite top**) Vehicles rendered immobile by Chinese fire or sub-zero temperatures were wheeled or shoved off the road to allow the column to pass. (**Opposite bottom**) The apron bridge skirting a power station west of the Funchilin Pass had been a prime target of Chinese sappers who destroyed it twice only to have it repaired by Army engineers. Their third try necessitated 24-feet of bridging material— capable of supporting 46-ton tanks— to span a hole over the 1,500-foot-deep gorge. Without it, the 14,000 men in Kot'o-ri could still cross the narrow footpath above the station but their 1,200 vehicles would be lost. To do the job, eight 2-ton M2 treadway bridge sections were loaded one each into C-119 Flying Boxcars and parachuted to the engineers.

The last elements of the 1st Marine and 7th Infantry Division from the Chosin reservoir reached the safety of the 3d Infantry Division lines at Chinhung-ni on Monday, 11 December 1950. (**Opposite**) A 3d Infantry Division mortar team preparing a meal of boiled rice in their foxhole, Thursday, 7 December.

Casualties among the American soldiers and Marines, ROK troops serving as Katusas and British Royal Marines fighting alongside their American counterparts had topped 10,500 during the breakout. (**Above**) The need to use all available space on vehicles and planes for the evacuation of wounded, plus the lack of time to conduct individual burials, necessitated that 117 American, Korean and British fighting men be interred in a common grave scratched out of the frozen earth near a 155-mm. battery at Kot'o-ri, Friday, 8 December. The remains were turned over to the United Nations representatives after the 1953 cease-fire.

During the breakout, the X Corps constructed a formidable, layered defensive perimeter around Hamhung, Yonpo Airfield and the port of Hungnam to cover its evacuation. As it turned out, however, the CCF in northeast Korea was a spent force that had suffered at least 70-percent casualties to all causes. The piecemeal efforts of CCF and reconstituted NKPA units to penetrate the Hamhung Perimeter were broken up with relative ease by massed UN firepower. Seventh Infantry Division 155-mm. self-propelled howitzers (**above**) and infantry defense position (**opposite top**) north of Hamhung near Sinhung, Saturday, 2 December 1950. M46 Pattons of the 3d Infantry Division (**opposite bottom**) deployed behind a dyke outside Kagae-dong for additional protection, Thursday, 7 December 1950.

Marine F4U Corsairs and, in the background to the right, Marine C-47s and Air Force F-51 Mustangs at Yonpo Airfield, early December 1950. With unexpended rockets, the Corsair in the foreground taxies in from a sortie for refueling and rearming before taking off on another mission. (**Below**) 7th Infantry Division soldiers after moving back to a defense line within Hamhung, Friday, 15 December. (**Opposite top**) LSTs ashore on Green Beach and barrels of aviation fuel on Dock No. 4 as seen from a ship berthed in Hungnam harbor, Monday, 11 December. (**Opposite bottom**) The high speed transport USS *Begor* lies at anchor to help cover the last troop withdrawals as Hungnam's harbor installations are ripped apart by huge explosions, Sunday, 24 December.

Accompanying the retreat of UN forces from North Korea was the mass migration of nearly three million civilians who's primary motive appeared to be fear of the Chinese. Fleeing to the south by ship, rail and foot in fantastic numbers, their movement severely complicated the Eighth Army's logistical problems and constrained its mobility. (**Opposite**) A seemingly endless file of refugees slogs through the snow near the east coast city of Kangnung and down a pass east of Seoul, early January 1951. (**Above**) ROK recruits prepare to leave Taegu Station for the front, Monday, 18 December 1950.

Men of the 24th Infantry Division enjoying a not-so-merry Christmas dinner near Puchon, south of the 38th Parallel and (**opposite top**) retreating toward Seoul three days into the CCF's New Year's offensive. Seoul was abandoned to the Communists the following day, Thursday, 4 January 1951. (**Opposite bottom**) 7th Infantry Division artillery firing on NKPA troops near Tanyang in the central mountains, Tuesday, 16 January 1951. To their left was the 2d Infantry, which had recently been forced to abandon the important road center at Wonju.

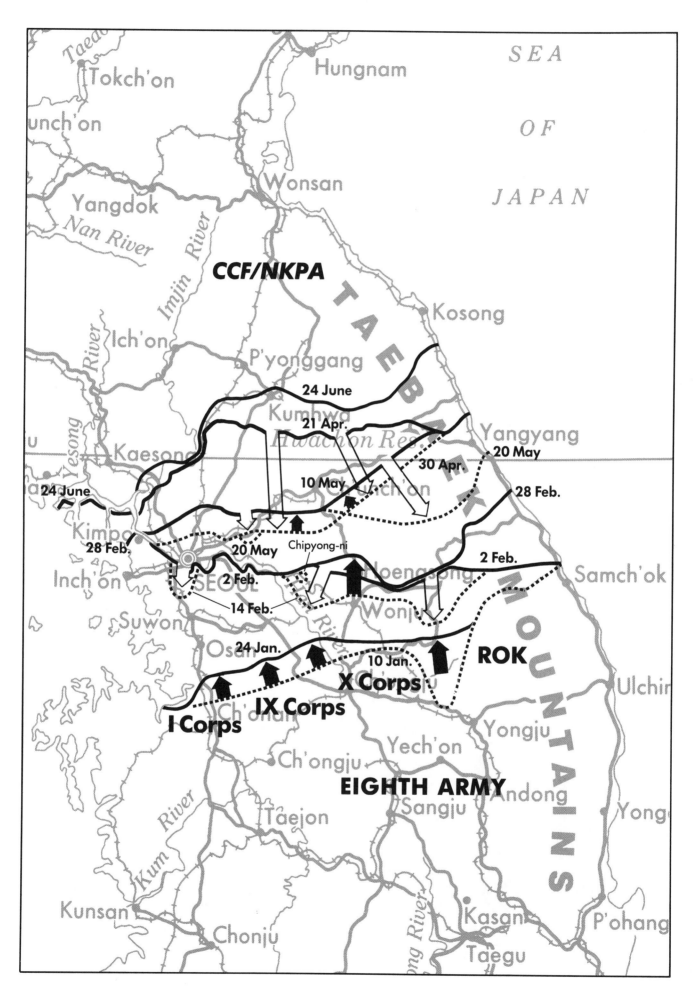

SEA

OF

JAPAN

Tokch'on

Hungnam

unch'on

Yangdok

Nan River

Wonsan

CCF/NKPA

Ich'on

P'yonggang

Kosong

Kumhwa

24 June

Hwachon Res.

21 Apr.

Yangyang

Kaesong

20 May

30 Apr.

24 June

10 May

28 Feb.

Kimpo

28 Feb.

20 May   Chipyong-ni

2 Feb.

Samch'ok

Inch'on

SEOUL

2 Feb.

Hoengsong

Suwon

14 Feb.

Wonju

Osan

24 Jan.

ROK

Ulchir

IX Corps

10 Jan.

X Corps

I Corps

Ch'o

Yongju

Yech'on

EIGHTH ARMY

Ch'ongju

Sangju

Andong

Yong

Taejon

Kum River

Kasan

Kunsan

P'ohang

Chonju

Taegu

CHAPTER SIX

Attacks and Counterattacks

Matthew B. Ridgway assumed command of UN ground forces on Tuesday, 26 December 1950. Three days earlier, Ridgway's predecessor, Walton H. Walker, had been killed when his jeep collided with an ROK truck on an icy road. The new commander arrived to find both his army and his boss in Tokyo severely shaken by the events of the previous month and a fatigued MacArthur told him, "the Eighth Army is yours, Matt. Do what you think best." Ridgway immediately moved to instill a winning spirit in his demoralized troops. As soon as the momentum of the Communist's offensive slowed in mid-January, he ordered that all units probe north to reestablish contact with the CCF and reconstituted NKPA. Soldiers who had grown used to "bugging out" initially were wary of the new gung ho general and the name "Wrong-way Ridgway" spread quickly throughout the ranks.

But Ridgway knew how to lead men in battle. Much to the distress of his headquarters staff in Taegu, he spent most of his time with front line units where his confidence and combative spirit went far towards transforming the UN forces into a winning team. In a three month long series of deliberate, limited-objective operations bearing such names as THUNDERBOLT, PUNCH, ROUNDUP, RIPPER and KILLER, he edged the Eighth Army north; not in great corps or division sized drives down main road nets (which invariably left thousands of dangerous guerrillas in the army's wake), but literally battalion by battalion. A hill or town would be taken in a set piece assault utilizing a heavy artillery preparation, air strikes and tank support. Then, other units would be quickly brought up on the flanks, sweeping all enemy forces before them prior to the next jump-off.

General Collins had arrived from the US in time to witness Ridgway's first effort, a well-coordinated reconnaissance in force named WOLFHOUND, and left with the conviction that, "the Eighth Army can take care of itself." Collins' visit marked the end of MacArthur's influence on US policy making. The gallant old general was pressing hard to obtain four more Army divisions from the United States, stating unequivocally that he needed that many soldiers just to stabilize the front. Ridgway, however, clearly had the situation well in hand without the additional troops and was confident that the 365,000 men under his command could not only hold their own, but push the half million or so CCF and NKPA troops back across the Parallel. The JCS began to deal directly with Ridgway, bypassing his Far East commander in chief.

The Eighth Army's attacks continued through February and March as thawing snow, heavy rains and the guerrilla forces left behind during the previous year's drive from Pusan to the Parallel severely hampered the resupply of front-line units. A Communist counteroffensive from 11 to 18 February temporarily checked the UN advance but was beaten back with the CCF suffering brutal losses in what some GIs called "the Wonju turkey shoot." On the west side of the Communist's breakthrough, a surrounded regi-

ment of the 2d Infantry Division and its attached French battalion * stubbornly clung to the key road junction of Chip'yong-ni and repulsed massed attacks by three CCF divisions until reinforced by a regiment of the 1st Cavalry Division. Below Chip'yong-ni, and west of Wonju, a 12-mile gash in the UN lines was plugged by the ROK 6th Division and the 27th British Commonwealth Brigade while, to the east, the US 7th and badly battered ROK 3d and 5th Divisions managed to hold Chech'on.

Once the offensive had spent itself, Ridgway's forces attacked, giving the Communists no time to reorganize. The entire central and eastern part of the line collapsed by 1 March. When the Han River was crossed near Seoul, CCF supply lines in the west became endangered and the Chinese suddenly pulled back rather than risk encirclement. The South Korean capital was retaken with little fighting on Thursday, 15 March. A week later, the 187th Airborne Regimental Combat Team conducted an airdrop near the key road and rail center of Munsan-ni. But like the parachute landings outside P'yongyang the previous year, it failed to bag many retreating enemy. March 1951 drew to a close with UN troops continuing their careful, northward sweep through the rain and mud as the CCF and NKPA pulled back above the Parallel to organize another offensive.

To keep the enemy off balance and meet his offensive as far north as possible, Ridgway continued to press the attack and moved his forces across the Parallel into territory he viewed as favorable defensive ground. On 12 April he issued Plan AUDACIOUS which was designed to let the steam out of the Communist's initial surge and bring the maximum amount of air and artillery fire power down on them. AUDACIOUS outlined an orderly, fighting withdrawal through carefully chosen phase lines and minimized the chances that a large UN unit would be cut off and decimated. It was to be Ridgway's last field order to the Eighth

*The French Battalion was commanded by Lieutenant Colonel Ralph Monclar who gave up his four-star rank of *General de Corps d' Armee* to take the unit to Korea. The battalion's men would later form the core of a highly mobile regimental task force in Vietnam named *Groupement Mobile 100* which was destroyed in a series of road ambushes in June 1954.

Army before he was directed to take command of all forces in the Far East.

MacArthur's defiance of his commander in chief had finally cost him his job. A series of public statements by the general undercut President Truman's peace initiative and made it plain that he was in complete disagreement with the handling of the war. On the recommendation of the Joint Chiefs of Staff, the President stripped him of all commands and ordered him home. Truman later explained: "General MacArthur was ready to risk general war. I was not." Army Secretary Frank Pace was in Korea when the decision was made to relieve MacArthur. After breaking the news to Ridgway that he was to take over as chief of the Far East and UN commands, Pace asked: "Now do we congratulate each other or shoot ourselves?"

Lieutenant General James A. Van Fleet had been in command of the Eighth Army for only a week when the Communists welcomed him with a massive, two-phase assault utilizing 487,000 CCF and NKPA troops. The initial drive was mounted from the Iron Triangle, their major assembly and supply area, and quickly spread along the front with a strong effort toward Seoul. Although the weight of the attack broke the ROK 6th Division near the UN line's center, the neighboring 24th Infantry and 1st Marine Divisions secured their flanks and the planned fighting withdrawal was accomplished with remarkably few casualties. A Gloucestershire battalion of the British 29th Brigade was, however, overrun when the ROK 1st Division on its flank was pushed back in heavy fighting. Survivors of the battalion eventually made their way back to UN lines after breaking out in a *northward* attack which took the encircling Chinese by surprise.

As expected, the CCF adhered to their doctrine that divisions should be committed to combat for about six days before being withdrawn to replenish supplies and replace casualties. The Chinese offensive lost momentum after five days and they retired north out of artillery range. This time, however, they were followed closely by UN forces who made every effort to stay in contact with the withdrawing enemy. The Communists then shifted the weight of their attack to the east. The X Corps' US 2d, ROK 5th and ROK 7th divisions held firm, as did the ROK I Corps, but the ROK III Corps between them was shattered. General Van Fleet had expected the renewed assault to come in this area and had already shifted his reserves into place. The 3d Infantry Division and 187th Airborne Regimental Combat Team were thrown forward to blunt the penetration as the 2d Infantry and 1st Marine Divisions attacked from the west.

The collapse of the Communists' largest and costliest offensive of the war brought about a general UN advance on all fronts and by Saturday, 2 June, UN forces were back along the same ground they had held in mid-April. Communist losses during May totalled a staggering 166,000 men, 37,000 of them to just the 2d Infantry Division which itself suffered 900 casualties including 134 soldiers killed. At one point the 2d had been almost surrounded and even their main supply route had been blocked, but long and hard experience had taught the division that it was safer to hold fast against the initial Chinese surge than to attempt to cut its way through in a hasty withdrawal.

As the first year of the war neared an end, it was apparent that the Eighth Army would have experienced little trouble driving north to establish a shorter line at the peninsula's narrow waist. Unfortunately, all of the potential stop lines were located along terrain which contained few of the natural defenses offered by the current position. Moreover, the roads leading north were poor, and as UN supply lines lengthened, the Communists' would shorten. Van Fleet, who had originally wanted to invest the Iron Triangle and capture Wonsan, decided instead to establish a strong defense line along the ground his soldiers occupied. The only advances to be made would be local in character to improve the Eighth Army's position and keep the Communists off balance.

The Chinese, meanwhile, were facing mounting problems at home as well as in the war. Thwarted in their efforts to establish air bases in North Korea by UN airpower, having suffered nearly a half million casualties since November, and beginning to feel the pinch of a widely supported UN embargo, Chinese leaders were now willing to sit down and discuss an armistice, if only to gain some breathing space and time to reorganize their forces.

On 1 June, UN Secretary General Trygve Lie stated that a cease-fire in the general vicinity of the 38th Parallel would fulfill that body's objectives. Discreet negotiations were quickly begun between the Soviets and Americans and on 23 June, Soviet UN Ambassador Jacob Malik announced his government's cease-fire proposal. At both the diplomatic and military levels, arrangements for the opening of negotiations moved quickly and, on Thursday, 5 July, UN representatives held the first meeting with their Chinese and North Korean counterparts in a Kaesong teahouse. Along the front, troops were fortifying the positions won during Operation PILEDRIVER, an offensive which succeeded in pushing the battle lines within one to ten miles south of where they would stand after two more years of fighting.

Elements of the 3d Infantry Division's largely Puerto Rican 65th Regimental Combat Team moving out toward Osan in Operation WOLFHOUND, Ridgway's first major attempt to maintain constant contact with— and pressure on— the CCF, Monday, 15 January 1951. The success of this relatively small operation was to have far-reaching consequences for General of the Army Douglas MacArthur's ability to influence strategic planning. (**Below**) A convoy of the 2d Infantry Division jammed up on an icy road south of Wonju, Wednesday, 10 January. The division, which had been savagely battered a little over a month before at Kunu-ri, defied all NKPA efforts to force it from its positions until the disintegration of the ROK III Corps on the 2d's right forced a withdrawal. (**Opposite top**) Ridgway and MacArthur visiting the 25th Infantry Division's front after its capture of Suwon, Sunday, 28 January. (*Left to right*) MacArthur's radioman, maintaining contact with Far East headquarters, and aide-de-camp, Brigadier General Courtney Whitney; Ridgway; Lieutenant Colonel Gilbert J. Check, Commander, 27th Infantry Regiment; Major General William B. Kean, Commander, 25th Infantry Division (*in background*); and MacArthur. (**Opposite bottom**) Ridgway with Major James H. Lee, a 25th Infantry Division battalion commander, and the division's Deputy Commander, Brigadier General Joseph Bradley, Monday, 5 February.

By the latter part of January, UN forces had begun systematic probing to the north. (**Above**) The crew of a 3d Infantry Division M19 dual-40 view the burning town of Chamsil-li on the Hahn River's south bank, Sunday, 20 January 1951. Throughout the month, however, persistent guerrilla activities required constant vigilance behind the lines. (**Opposite top**) Members of the X Corps' Special Activities Group return the fire of Communist guerrillas in the hills above Mun'gyong-ni, Monday, 15 January. (**Opposite bottom**) Marines getting ready to move against guerrilla bastions in the eastern Taebaek Mountains in HRS-1 helicopters. The 1st Marine Division was pulled from the Eighth Army's reserve to counter a North Korean division which had infiltrated ROK lines during the Communist's mid-January offensive and turned to guerrilla activities in the area bounded generally by the upland cities of Andong and Uisong and the coastal cities of Yongdok and P'ohang-dong. Unfortunately, few helicopters were available to speed the work of Marines conducting "rice paddy patrols" and operations dragged well into February.

As January came to a close, the Eighth Army moved methodically forward in deliberate, limited-objective attacks. (**Opposite**) The lead riflemen of a 1st Cavalry Division unit fan out under the watchfull eyes of another unit moving behind them on Friday, 26 January 1951, and (**opposite bottom**) a Chinese prisoner taken by the division. (**Above**) Phosphorous shells exploding on Communist positions in the 25th Infantry Division area, Thursday, 1 February.

25th Infantry Division troops advancing toward Seoul and Inch'on during Operation PUNCH. (**Opposite top**) Soldiers entering the outskirts of Anyang-ni on Tuesday, 6 February 1951 and (**opposite bottom**) moving through Yongdungp'o on Friday, 9 February. (**Top**) A pair of infantrymen cautiously work their way through a burning village and (**above**) Major Logan E. Weston briefs his men before moving out on Tuesday.

Lieutenant General Matthew B. Ridgway leaving Kimpo Airport, where he had just landed, to assume command of the Eighth Army, Wednesday, 27 December 1950. Seated behind him is Colonel William A. Collier from the Eighth Army's advance headquarters in Seoul. Unlike Collier and the other occupants of the jeep, Ridgway lacked adequate winter gear for several days after rushing to Korea from the United States.

Ridgway's War

On 9 May 1984, General Matthew B. Ridgway, US Army (Ret.), addressed the students and faculty of the Army's Command and General Staff College at Fort Leavenworth, Kansas, during a seminar on leadership. After a very brief opening statement, General Ridgway, then 89, stood for questions for approximately two hours. Below are some of the comments of this great captain whose inspired leadership was instrumental in preventing the defeat of UN forces after China's entry into the Korean War. A more complete transcript can be found in the May 1990 edition of the US Army's professional journal, Military Review.

"I had the great advantage of having been deputy chief of staff in Washington and had followed the Korean operation for 14 hours a day from the time of the outbreak of that invasion on the 25th of June until I left in December. So I was thoroughly familiar, as far as one could be that distance from the theater, with what was going on there and I

knew the commanders and so forth . . . I did not come into something cold. What I did not know was the feeling of the commanders in the field . . .

"The very first thing to do was visit [them] in the field, personally, and make each commander brief his situation, on the ground. Then you can get a good idea of what his state of mind is. Is he confident, does he know what he is doing, does he know the terrain in his area? Then you talk to as many enlisted men as you can. That all took some days. But within 48 hours or so, I had visited every corps and division commander, except one way over on the east coast."

"The next big thing was to restore the spirit of the army. It had been badly handled, tactically, logistically and really spiritually. It had been committed to action at a time when the forces in Japan were about as unprepared for combat as an army could be. I guess you all know the circumstances . . . The enlisted men had people to shine their shoes and did not do any KP . . . and all sorts of things like that. But most of all, it was an attitude of mind . . .

"The lack of cooperation between the adjacent units was deplorable. When I would go up front to visit the battalions, as soon as I got up there, I said: 'Your infantry predecessors would roll over in their graves the way you've been conducting operations here. You are road bound; you cannot get off the road. You say you don't have communications . . . you have got runners, use them. Get up in the hills and take the high ground.' They got mousetrapped there, time and time again, by advancing down these narrow little valleys. They did not want to climb steep knife ridges."

"**When you go in** to take over a new command, particularly at a time when the situation was as it was then— the troops were confused . . . they didn't know just what was going on— you must be very careful about how a new broom sweeps clean . . . You must tread softly. I had three rules that I followed with respect to relieving an officer in battle . . . First, I must know him and what he had done over a sufficient length of time by personal observation up in his own area. Second, what would be the effect on his unit if he were relieved? I have in mind one very fine example: the men just loved this man, they thought highly of him, there wasn't anything wrong with him except he was just mediocre and you do not want mediocre leadership when the lives of so many men are at stake. The third requisite was that I have someone else on hand who was better, to put in place right away . . .

"I had to relieve two division commanders. You do it on the basis of your own personal knowledge, not second hand reports . . . If you have been up there with him in the crisis of action, you see how he operates and what his degree of confidence is. Then it makes it easy to reach your decision, but by and large I took a long time . . . Some of these commanders were tired. They had been through the whole thing since June. One man had a very painful back, and I could sympathize with him because I had that trouble myself for years."

"**These division commanders** did not know the terrain. I remember asking one man the names of very prominent peaks in his own sector. He did not know them. He did not even know the name of the river that ran through his sector. I asked about the ground over there: 'Is that feasible for armor?' Well, he did not know that either . . . In the presence of their staffs, at least their general staffs, I would express confidence . . . whether I felt that way or not. When you take over in an emergency like that you just can't sweep them out, your effect may be devastating. The main thing to do is to build confidence, and then you allow it to grow.

"Another thing I wanted to do was to get the two corps to cooperate. They were not doing it. The I and IX Corps were the only two I had on line; the X Corps was still at sea. They did not have sufficient cooperation, intimate contact, patrols or anything. Those are the first things you get to, but most of all, the basic thing was to restore the confidence of the troops. The fighting spirit will come with it."

"**All of this business** of restoring the fighting spirit; it is a multitude of little details, gentlemen. The synergistic effect over a long time is what works the miracles on them. If you stop and ask these men, stop and talk to senior noncommissioned officers, you find out, little by little, what is on their minds. Take immediate steps to remedy a problem, if it should be remedied. I asked one man what was his particular gripe. He wanted to write home, but never got any stationary to write on. So I had somebody send up a supply of stationary that night to the unit marked for this soldier. That word gets around . . . Go to the hospital and visit the men there. Go to the commanding officer of the hospital and ask how the nurses are treating the patients; are they instilling in them the intense desire to get back to their unit? One replacement there, who has been wounded and comes back to his own unit, back with his own buddies— he's worth four or five of the men who have come 9,000 miles . . . There's just a lot of little tiny details, but the sum of them is what counts."

"**Within 48 hours** you could be pulled out of your comfortable home here in the United States and be in combat. I had less than 24 hours' notice to leave, to take over command . . . I had my combat clothes on, but I did not have any gloves. I had civilian gloves and did not have anything but a cotton cap. I nearly froze there the first few days, until some major saw me one day holding my ears, and he went in and got me one of these pile-lined caps with the flaps and a pair of GI gloves . . . Any soldier up there sure would like to have a pair of gloves, you know, when the temperature is down below or around zero and his hands are cold and raw."

"**To me, a basic element** in troop leadership is the responsibility of the commander to be where the crisis of action is going to happen. He does not belong back at his command post and I would say that goes right on down the line . . . Certainly you don't want to be the lead scout [but] I think the commander should be where the going is toughest. He is not there to trespass on the sphere of his subordinates. He is there to drink in, by his senses and all his experience, the actual situation, the human element above all else."

Australian soldiers of the British Commonwealth Brigade giving covering fire to troops pinned down in front of enemy positions. (**Opposite**) 1st Cavalry Division MPs mopping up Chinese stragglers after Operation KILLER on Tuesday, 27 February 1951 (*top*) and Thursday, 5 March. Note the sniper rifle being used by one of the MPs.

Task forces from the 25th Infantry Division secured Kimpo Air Base and Inch'on harbor on Saturday, 10 February 1951, and Seoul City Air Base (**above**) the following day. All of these facilities, however, had been severely damaged by Eighth Army demolition teams when UN forces evacuated in early January and then again when the Communists pulled out. Although it would take time to get the port and air bases operating at full capacity, the area was now firmly under UN control and I Corps troops could look across the wide Han River at their next objective, Seoul.

(**Below**) Tank crewmen examine the disabled left track of their M4 Sherman moments after it hit a mine on the outskirts of Hadaewa, Wednesday, 28 February. The area is coming under some small arms fire and accompanying infantrymen keep a watchful eye for enemy troops. (**Opposite top**) 3d Infantry Division soldiers flatten themselves against the sides of a draw as enemy mortar rounds explode nearby, Tuesday, 13 February. North Korean forces were counterattacking I Corps from their bridgehead on the south bank of the Han River. (**Opposite bottom**) One of the 3d's dual-40 anti-aircraft guns firing on Chinese positions across the Han River in Seoul, Sunday, 4 March.

(**Opposite**) Under the protection of one of the largest artillery preparations of the war, 25th Infantry Division men and tanks cross the Han River near its confluence with the Pukhan, Wednesday, 7 March 1951. To the west, the 3d Infantry Division and ROK 1st Division conducted diversionary operations to draw the enemy's attention away from the 25th's effort. The bridgehead was vigorously contested until Friday night when the Communists conducted a skillful withdrawal from the area. (**Above**) A DUKW-353 "Duck" ferries troops across the Han River near Seoul, Friday, 16 March. The pulverized remains of the capital had changed hands for the fourth—and last— time the day before.

Propaganda leaflets produced by the Eighth Army's Psychological Warfare Section are handed to a pilot who will drop them over Communist positions. Sometimes the leaflets would be of a general nature like the English language side of the safe conduct pass at right. On other occasions, they would be geared to support specific campaigns or capitalize on a developing situation along the front. For example, when CCF and NKPA units in the hills around Wonju and Chech'on were found to have suffered catastrophic losses from artillery fire and air strikes in February and March of 1951, Communist units retreating from the area received leaflets with the terse invitation: "Count your men!"

(**Opposite**) Leaflets dropped by Fifth Air Force bombers over North Korean population centers. Modeled after the successful propaganda campaign aimed at Japanese civilians during the waning days of World War II, they were designed to undermine the authority of the Communist government and disrupt its war economy by encouraging civilians to move away from the cities. The top leaflet warns that "fighters and bombers will soon destroy ALL military targets along the railroads and highways outlined in red on the map . . ." and ends with instructions to "Leave this danger area IMMEDIATELY!!" Only the marked targets would, in fact, be bombed, thus increasing the credibility and effectiveness of future propaganda efforts. The bottom leaflet reads in part: "If you and your loved ones live in or near these targets, leave immediately, the bombing attacks will start soon. If the Communists will not let you leave, send your families to safety. Warn your friends to do the same . . ." The leaflet ends with a plea to "Flee to safety now! Save your lives!"

EIGHTH
UNITED STATES ARMY

"OFFICIAL EIGHTH ARMY SAFE CONDUCT PASS"

It is hereby ordered that accomodations and good treatment be given to the bearer of this certificate and his followers. They have voluntarily disarmed themselves, ceased resistance, and surrender to the UN forces in accordance with proper procedure.

BY COMMAND OF LIEUTENANT GENERAL RIDGWAY:

OFFICIAL:

R. L. Butt Jr
R. L. BUTT Jr
Lt. Col. AGC
Acting Adjutant General

LEVEN C. ALLEN
Maj Gen, GSC
Chief of Staff

EUSAK 8513 CHINESE

경고

철로와 큰 길 가에 있는 모든 군사목표는 유엔공군의 폭격을 받을 것이다.

만포 · 강계 · 신의주 · 구성 · 정주 · 희천 · 구장 · 신안주 · 순천 · 성천 · 양덕 · 평양 · 진남포 · 겸이포 · 영흥 · 원산 · 함흥 · 사리원 · 장연

1205

목숨을 살리라 !

유엔공군의 전투기와 폭격기는 머지않어 철로와 큰 길 …지도 위에 빨간줄을 친 곳 가에 있는 모든 군사목표를 분쇄하고야 말 것이다. 이 군사목표란 일반시민들의 집안에 감추어둔 군수품, 혹은 뒷골목에 숨겨둔 하물찬 또는 무엇이 들었는지 공산군 장병들을. 유엔군은 항공사진으로 군사목표를 다 알고 있다.

이 경고대로하면 살 수 있다 !!

그곳에서 곧 떠나라 ! 갖출을 달리고 갈것이며 동무에게도 알리라 — 만일 공산도배들이 여러분을 위험한 지역에 강제로 남아있게 한들 부대와 전차 등 일로 유엔군은 북한 일반시민들이 피해를 입지 않기를 원한다 …… 여러분은 이 경고대로하여 목숨을 살리라 !

이 위험지구에서 곧 떠나라 !!

1205

8484 5 A.C.

경고

병 사 · 수송기관 · 군수품 · 수선공장

1204

이 경고를 귀담아 들으라 !

유엔공군이 공산군의 모든 군사시설물과 군사물품을 철부지고야 말 것이다. …이것이 어디에 있는 것을 유엔공군으로 잘 알고 있었다. 중공군과 김일성군인 군수품과 수선공장과 심지어는 병사들까지도 일반 북한주민들의 집안에 이용시키고 감추고 왔다는 것을 유엔 공군이 찍어 알고 있다. 유엔공군이 찍어 항공사진이 이것을 증명하고 있다.

유엔군은 일반시민을 상하게할 의사가 조금도 없다 그러나 공산군의 모든 군사목표를 분쇄 않을수 없을 것이다

이 경고를 귀담아 들으라 !

유엔공군은 결망 일반시민들에게 피해를 주죠삼지는 않는다. 그러나 전쟁을 일부러 끌며 무고한 백성들의 집안을 이용함으로 군수품을 쌓고있는 공산군을 그대로 둘수는 없다. 만일 누군가 이러한 군사목표안에서나 또는 가까이 상있으면 곧 피난하라. 유엔군의 폭격은 곧 시작될 것이다.

이 경고를 귀담아 들으라 !

귀한 목숨을 지금이다 ! 피난할때는 지금이다 !

1204

By the last week of March, 1951, UN forces were closing on the 38th Parallel along most of the front. (**Above**) An endless column of 3d Infantry Division troops and South Korean porters moves to positions near the village of Uijong-hu and (**below**) a 24th Infantry Division patrol in the Chugyong-san area, Friday, 23 March. (**Opposite**) A C-47 cargo plane of the Royal Hellenic Air Force takes off from an advance airstrip as a 105-mm. howitzer pounds CCF troop concentrations four miles to the north.

In an effort to catch retreating Communists before they could cross the Imjin River, the 187th Airborne Regimental Combat Team and two Ranger companies parachuted into drop zones at Munsan-ni, roughly 20 miles northwest of Seoul, on Friday, 23 March 1951. (**Clockwise**) Paratroopers check their gear before boarding some of the 135 C-119 transports launching the operation from Taegu; the drop; and paratroopers cross a field under fire. Most enemy units in the area had already escaped to the north when the drop occurred and barely 300 casualties were inflicted on the NKPA. Captured North Korean soldiers stated that they had been told to expect an air drop and it is likely that a general warning was issued to all Communist forces after the huge concentration of aircraft flown to Taegu from Japan was sighted by espionage agents observing the airfield.

On Wednesday, 11 April 1951, General of the Army Douglas MacArthur was relieved of all commands and replaced by Lieutenant General Matthew B. Ridgway after making a series of public statements which undercut a Presidential peace initiative and openly displayed his deep disagreement with the administration's policies. Virtually all of the President's close advisors and the Joint Chiefs of Staff backed the dismissal— with varying degrees of enthusiasm— and Secretary of Defense George C. Marshall believed it was long overdue. (**Opposite**) MacArthur, his wife Jean and son Arthur depart the Capitol after his address to a joint session of Congress, Thursday, 19 April. MacArthur, who told the assembled body: "Old soldiers never die they just fade away," did anything but fade as he launched into a busy, nation-wide speaking tour and made an unsuccessful bid for the 1952 Republican nomination for President.

(**Above**) President Harry S Truman and his principal advisors after the Wake Island meeting with MacArthur: (*left to right*) special presidential envoy Averell Harriman, Marshall, Truman, Secretary of State Dean Acheson, Secretary of the Treasury John W. Snyder, Ambassador at Large Philip C. Jessup (*behind Acheson and Snyder*), Secretary of the Army Frank Pace

and Chairman of the Joint Chiefs of Staff General Omar N. Bradley. Seated with Bradley in the Pentagon are the three service chiefs: (*left to right*) Air Force Chief of Staff General Hoyt S. Vandenberg, Bradley, Army Chief of Staff General J. Lawton Collins and Chief of Naval Operations Admiral Forrest P. Sherman.

The grim-faced group in the lower photo was clearly intimidated by MacArthur's stature as a military man with a great depth of experience in the Far East, his extreme popularity at home and his five-star rank. In August, 1950, when he was the Army's Deputy Chief of Staff, Ridgway had engaged in extensive talks with MacArthur and Averell Harriman in Tokyo. At a later meeting in the Pentagon with Marshall and the Joint Chiefs, Ridgway's suggestion that MacArthur be given orders like any other theater commander was followed by what he described as "a frightened silence." The subject was broached again as the meeting broke up and Vandenberg replied: "What good would that do? He wouldn't obey the orders. What can we do?" Ridgway later recalled that his reply: "You can relieve any commander who won't obey orders, can't you?" prompted a look of puzzled amazement from Vandenberg who then, simply, walked away.

Eighth Army troops along the 38th Parallel. (**Opposite top**) A paratrooper on Hill 148, east of Munsan-ni, Tuesday, 27 March 1951 and 25th Infantry Division soldiers near the Hant'an River on Wednesday, 11 April (**above**) and Wednesday, 28 March (**opposite bottom**). During this period, UN forces consolidated their positions along the border in anticipation of a massive spring offensive by the Communists and made few efforts to fight their way into the thick band of fortifications that the North Koreans had constructed before the war. After the CCF and NKPA expended a remarkable 166,000 men in a failed, two-phase offensive which opened on Sunday, 22 April, the Eighth Army moved through the fortifications with little difficulty and were well above the Parallel along most of its length by the end of May.

Men of a 3d Infantry Division reconnaissance company carry the body of one of their comrades killed in a firefight with Chinese troops near Songdong-dong, Sunday, 20 May 1951. **(Below)** Soldiers wounded near the Soyang River are loaded onto a military police truck by 2d Infantry Division medical personnel, Thursday, 31 May. **(Opposite)** A Marine forward air controller observes a strike on an enemy-held hill in the Soyang Valley south of Yanggu, Tuesday, 29 May.

Private Roman Prauty of the 7th Infantry Division attempts to shield his ears from the blast of an M20 75-mm. recoilless rifle. The weapon is being fired in support of infantry fighting across a valley in the Oet'ook-tong area, Saturday, 9 June 1951. (**Opposite top**) 24th Infantry Division riflemen east of Kumhwa, Wednesday, 20 June. (**Opposite bottom**) A wounded Thai soldier is given a drink at a 1st Cavalry Division aid station west of Yonch'on, Monday, 2 July.

Troops of the 3d Infantry Division's largely Puerto Rican 65th Regiment fight their way down a Chinese trench line east of Yonch'on, Friday, 1 June 1951. Note the fragmentation grenade lying ready for use in the foreground to the left of the trench. (**Opposite**) Eighth Army cannoneers reloading their 8-inch howitzer during a fire mission against Chinese targets, Sunday, 10 June 1951, and 24th Infantry Division troops top the crest of a hill, Wednesday, 20 June. Two soldiers in the foreground are armed with M2-2 flame throwers for reducing bunker positions. Tanked-up, they weighed up to 72 pounds and had a range of, roughly, 40 yards.

No sweeping war of movement, tankers in Korea found themselves operating almost exclusively in an infantry support role. (**Opposite top**) M46 Pershings of the 24th Infantry Division's tank battalion move into position prior to an assault on an enemy objective. Soldiers are barely visible in the tall grasses at the bottom of the photo. (**Opposite bottom**) An M4 Sherman just beyond the radio operator is almost completely obscured by the dust kicked up by its direct fire on Communist positions near Yanggu in the Hwach'on Reservoir area. Another agile Sherman has positioned itself well up slope of the next hill and Leatherneck riflemen can be seen silhouetted against the sky at upper right. (**Above**) 2d Infantry Division tanks move into position to support ROK 8th Division troops near Pia-ri, Sunday, 19 August.

South of P'yonggang in the Iron Triangle, a squad-sized group of infantry work their way cautiously across the saddle between Hill 717, which had just been captured, and well-camouflaged Chinese bunkers on the next hill. Back up Hill 717 to the left, other soldiers observe their progress and give covering small arms fire as does a machinegun crew in the right foreground. There may be at least one other squad working their way up the hill from another direction.

(**Opposite**) US and Katusa casualties on Hill 717. The soldier being treated in the foreground was hit in the face, arms and stomach by fragments from two grenades.

Because of the constrained nature of the terrain, attacks along a company "front" were often only wide enough to accommodate a single squad like the one above from the 3d Infantry Division's 1st Battalion, 7th Regimental Combat Team. Other squads coming in behind them would also give what-

ever support they could but the success of such attacks often boiled down to the expertise and determination of the men at the point of the spear.

Taking a hill was often a full-day affair— or more. Before sundown, US units would break off action and form a defensive perimeter somewhere on high ground and wait for the morning when daylight would bring them the full benefit of air and artillery cover. The Chinese, to minimize this advantage, conducted their counterattacks at night. Long lines of tommy-gunners, conspicuously silhouetted by the eerie light of flares and flashes of artillery bursts would rush hilltop positions. If the defenses could not be quickly overrun, groups of Chinese would fight from behind folds in the earth while others wormed their way through the brush and rocks to within grenade throwing range of the UN foxholes. The fighting would continue until just before dawn or until one side or the other ran out of ammunition and was forced to withdraw.

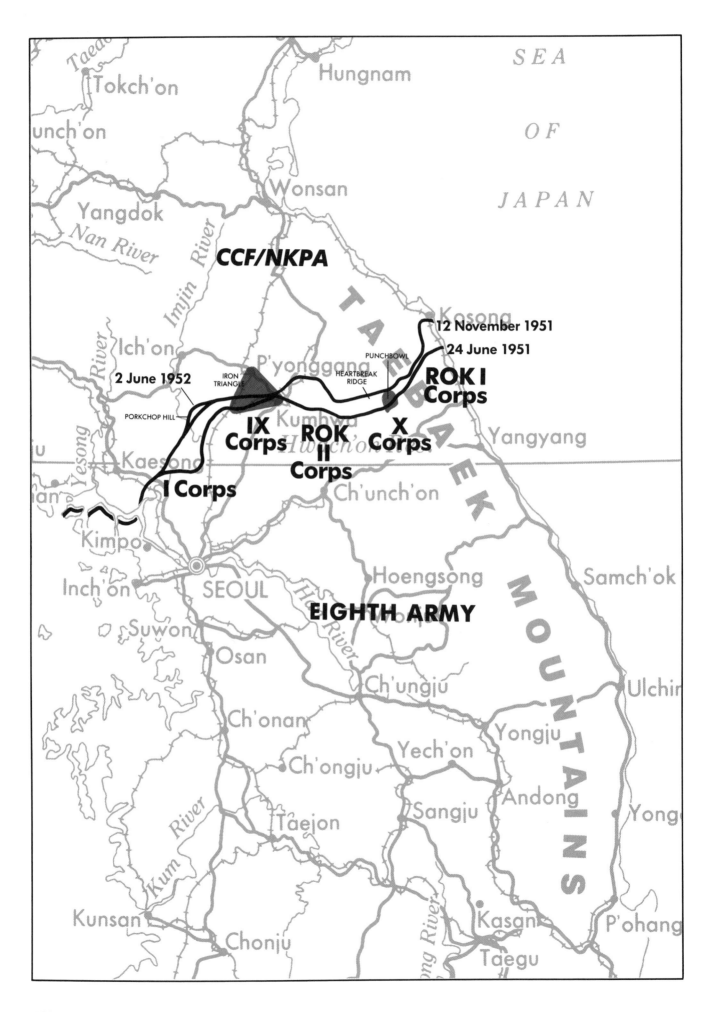

CHAPTER SEVEN

War Along the Outposts

Throughout the summer of 1951, Communist and United Nations forces engaged in bitter local fights to control ridges and hills as both sides attempted to adjust the front to their own advantage. Neither side was willing to undertake large-scale offensives while the truce talks were in progress and the Communists were additionally hampered by severe supply problems. General Van Fleet was satisfied with the outline of the front in July and felt that the Eighth Army could repel any assaults on its current position. The terrain was defensible and backed up by an adequate road and rail net, except in the rugged Taebaek Mountains. Van Fleet's seizure of the dominant hills at the base of the Iron Triangle also denied use of that important staging area to the enemy.

The front line remained almost stationary until late August when the recently opened truce talks were suspended by the UN command. The Kaesong negotiation site and its neutral zone were behind enemy lines and the Communists used its location to gain the maximum propaganda value by engaging in such activities as distributing photographs to foreign news agencies depicting UN representatives driving up under a white flag as proof that the United Nations was begging for terms. Repeated efforts were also made to intimidate the negotiators by herding them from place to place under armed guard and forcing them to sit in absurdly small chairs during the talks. When coupled with the fact that armed Chinese troops were being moved to the front through the safety of the neutral zone, it was obvious that the Communists had no intention of bargaining in good faith.

With the truce talks placed on hold, General Van Fleet took the opportunity to push the Communist forces further away from the Hwach'on Reservoir in the east, the Seoul-Ch'orwon railroad in the west and out of the heights above the Communists' supply center at Kumsong in the center. On Friday, 31 August, the 1st Marine Division attacked the northern rim of an area called the Punchbowl, a huge circular valley confined within sharp 1000 to 2000 ft. peaks. Two days later, the 2d Infantry Division reopened their assault on Bloody Ridge, roughly five miles southwest of the Marines' battle. The US 2d, ROK 5th and ROK 7th divisions had been trying to wrestle control of the western approaches to the Punchbowl since mid-August but had been unable to get a firm grip on Bloody Ridge and the adjacent hills until Tuesday, 4 September, the day after the Marines secured their initial objective.

After a week-long lull, the Marines struck north from the Punchbowl toward Hills 673 and 749, followed by a 2d Division drive to seize control of Heartbreak Ridge, a long hill mass which resembled the spinal column of a fish with dozens of vertebra-like ridges falling off to the east and west. What followed was some of the most intense fighting of the war as soldiers and Marines inched their way under fire up rocky slopes— lugging mortars, recoilless rifles, food and ammunition— to towering, knife-crested ridges. Throughout this fighting, the ROK I Corps recent seizure of a J-shaped ridge (aptly named J Ridge) five miles to the northeast enabled it to observe and fire upon North Korean reinforcements moving toward the Americans. Thousands of South Korean porters also brought up tons of critically needed supplies packed on to the sturdy, A-frame carriers strapped to their backs.

Meanwhile, above Seoul, the I Corps' five divisions pushed northwest along a forty-mile front to force the Chinese away from the rail line running to Ch'orwon and Kumhwa. The US 3d and 25th, ROK 1st and recently-formed British Commonwealth divisions met only light to moderate resistance on their way to the JAMESTOWN stop line, while the 1st Cavalry Division at the center of the advance was forced to fight through a deep web of bunkers and minefields for every inch of ground. The 1st Cav's front faced the Chinese supply base at Sangnyong-ni and over two-thirds of the 21,000 enemy casualties suffered during the UN's western drive were expended in their unsuccessful effort to halt the division's advance.

By the last week in October, all UN objectives in the east and west had been met and the capture of the commanding heights above Kumsong by the US 24th, ROK 2d and ROK 6th divisions brought an end to Korea's war of movement. Though nineteen months of self-imposed stalemate would pass before the front would see any significant realignments, Van Fleet's last push had been enough to convince the Communists to reopen armistice discussions.

On 12 November, General Ridgway ordered Van Fleet to cease offensive operations and to limit attacks to only those necessary to strengthen the main line of resistance (MLR). A series of heavily fortified outposts, manned at squad, platoon and even company strength were established one to three miles in front of the main trenches. From these highly vulnerable positions, UN forces sent out patrols to capture prisoners and determine enemy dispositions. The outposts were located within range of friendly artillery and would seriously impede any assault aimed at the MLR.

Only light, sporadic ground action occurred along the front during the winter of 1951-52, but behind the lines, great strides were made by the Communists in bringing forward modern, Soviet-built artillery which they managed to keep supplied with shells in spite of an extensive air interdiction effort. Ground activity increased dramatically in May, especially in the I Corps area at the west end of the MLR where the newly-arrived 45th Infantry Division* was repeatedly struck, and the ROK 1st Division repulsed over 30 Chinese probing attacks.

In an effort to effectively screen its front, the 45th pushed forward its outpost line into an area which would remain hotly contested until the armistice was signed more than a year later. At the southwest end of the Monday, 2 June assault, Old Baldy (Hill 266) and Porkchop Hill (Hill 255) fell to the Americans after heavy fighting while little opposition was encountered at the other end of the line on Arrowhead (Hill 281) and White Horse Hill (Hill 395) and six points inbetween. A seventh target, outpost Eerie (Hill 191), had been abandoned in March to the Chinese, who held out against the division until Saturday, 14 June. Throughout the month, virtually all of the newly won positions were subjected to frequent, determined counterattacks that were well-supported by the CCF's new artillery. Porkchop Hill and Old Baldy were the scenes of particularly violent actions.

I Corps struck back in July with the 45th, 1st Marine and ROK 1st divisions conducting individual raids deep into CCF territory northeast of the new armistice negotiation site at Panmunjon. Between the periodic, heavy rains of July and August, which brought all fighting to a standstill, both sides renewed their efforts to gain commanding ground.

Hill 58 changed hands five times in July before the 1st Marine Division was forced off for good. The Marines, however, then captured the neighboring— and dominant— Hill 122 in an assault which took the Chinese by surprise. The Marines held their ground against repeated counterattacks from 12 to 25 August and gave it the well-earned name of Bunker Hill.

Northeast of the Marines, the 2d Infantry Division took over the 45th's positions and was immediately thrown off Old Baldy on the night of 17-18 July. The division regained portions of the hill, as weather allowed, on Wednesday, 23 July, and Friday, 1 August; beating off the inevitable, violent counterattacks on each occasion. Old Baldy changed hands for the fourth time on Thursday, 18 September, as Chinese infiltrators fought their way through American trenches on the hill's crest. But two days later, the 2d again became king of the mountain when a tank-supported, two-

---

* The 40th and 45th Infantry Divisions were National Guard outfits that had arrived in Korea during the winter in order to relieve the 24th Infantry and 1st Cavalry Divisions which returned to their pre-war duties in Japan. The 40th Infantry Division had briefly occupied southern Korea after World War II.

pronged assault dislodged the Communists.

By October, the weight of the CCF effort moved to the northeast of the I Corps area as Arrowhead and White Horse Hill came under attack. Possession of these strategic hills would threaten the lateral road behind I Corps and the main supply route to Ch'orwon, now held by the 2d Infantry Division's French Battalion and elements of the ROK 9th Division. The French Battalion denied all Chinese efforts to drive them off Arrowhead during the week of 6-12 October and on Thursday, 9 October, the South Koreans fought their way back onto White Horse Hill after being forced to withdraw two days earlier.

An effort was made by the neighboring IX Corps to relieve the pressure on the defenders of White Horse and Arrowhead by seizing two large hill masses to their right. Hills 598 (Triangle Hill) and 500 lay in the southeast corner of the Iron Triangle and their possession by UN forces would also strengthen the defense of Kumhwa. The 7th and ROK 2d divisions opened their attack on the morning of Tuesday, October 14, and, in seesaw fighting which lasted the rest of the month, lost and regained their objectives several times.

The balance of the fighting before winter closed in again consisted mostly of raids and patrol clashes that often resulted in hundreds of Chinese or North Korean deaths. The I Corps area, however, continued to be the focus of the CCF's attention.

In the 1st Marine Division's sector, a low ridge called the Hook formed a deep salient poking north from the MLR. On Sunday, 26 October, the Chinese made a serious attempt to bite off the exposed position as the Hook and two adjacent outposts came under attack after a 48-hour artillery preparation. The Marines were driven from their positions in heavy fighting and did not regain full control of the area for two days. The Chinese made another effort to invest the Hook after the Marines turned the sector over to the British Commonwealth Division, but their 19 November assault met with even less success than the previous one. By year's end, both the Communist and UN forces had constructed defenses so strong that any attempt to capture them would exact a huge toll in blood and material.

A muddy British mortar crew lobs 4.2-inch shells across the Imjin River, early September 1951. British boys who grew up on tails of Flander's mud were able to go home and compare notes with their fathers after experienc-ing Korea's summer monsoons. (**Below**) M4A3 tanks, operating as artillery, have backed into excavated fire positions to give their relatively flat trajectory guns more elevation for greater range.

Platoon leader David H, Hackworth of the 25th Infantry Division shortly after his battlefield promotion to second lieutenant, early August 1950. The looted clock outside his command post bunker kept time for both friends— and foes on the next ridge— by sounding every hour on the hour. (**Below**) Marines firing a light 30-caliber machinegun have already expended two boxes of ammunition on nearby Communist positions.

2d Infantry Division soldiers look towards NKPA positions across the valley after nearly three weeks of fighting to gain control of Bloody Ridge in the Taebaek Mountains, Thursday, 6 September 1951. (**Opposite**) The division's troops spread along Hill 983, the crest of Bloody Ridge.

A 24th Infantry Division aid station in the Kumhwa–Sangnyong-ni Sector, Friday, 21 September 1951. (**Below**) Southwest of Ch'orwon, Corporal Charles R. Buckner of the 1st Cavalry Division returns from an unsuccessful attempt to find his platoon leader, Lieutenant Tubbs, missing after the unit went to aid a nearby company caught in an ambush, Sunday, 23 September.

(**Above**) Porters lugging 105-mm shells on A-frame carriers to an artillery unit in the mountains. The lack of any road system in the Bloody Ridge-Punchbowl area necessitated that the Eighth Army supplement airdrops by employing thousands of Koreans to move supplies forward. A widely circulated story related how, when a young boy arrived at a battery position, exhausted from a two-day journey with a shell strapped to his back, he was directed to a gun which immediately fired off the round. He was then told to turn around and get another— and he did, again and again. Other versions of this story existed and it showed up again nearly two decades later in Vietnam. Then, the porter was a North Vietnamese and the route was the somewhat lengthier Ho Chi Minh Trail.

The fact that it could take four men up to ten hours to get a stretcher case to an aid station was, however, anything but funny. An entire Marine transport squadron of 15 Sikorsky HRS-1 helicopters arrived at Sohwa-ri, east of the Punchbowl, on Monday, 10 September 1951, and was immediately put to work moving supplies and evacuating casualties. Within weeks, the helicopters were also lifting company-sized units into remote battle areas and, on Thursday, 11 October, managed to move a whole battalion.

"Red legs" of Battery C, 936th Field Artillery Battalion fire their 100,001st shell of the war at CCF positions near Ch'orwon, Tuesday, 10 October 1951. (**Opposite**) Long Toms firing in support of the 25th Infantry Division near Munema on the west central front, Sunday, 26 November.

In order to make up for the shortage of artillery in Korea (divisions had only about a quarter of the cannons that had been available to them in 1944-45) the Eighth Army's commander, Lieutenant General James A. Van Fleet gave his artillery battalions blanket authorization to exceed all prior limitations on fire. The result, was that gun crews began to place what was called a "Van Fleet load"— up to five times the normal amount of ordinance— on targets. Ammunition stocks began to run down quickly and budget-watchers in both the Congress and the Pentagon were appalled at the cost.

While not convinced that the Army's artillery was being used in the most efficient manner, General Ridgway, in October 1951, defended his subordinant to the Joint Chiefs by stating that: "Whatever may have been the impression of our operations in Korea to date, artillery has been and remains the great killer of Communists. It remains the great saver of soldiers, American and Allied. There is a direct relation between the piles of shells in the ammunition supply points and the piles of corpses in the graves registration collecting points. The bigger the former, the smaller the latter and vice versa." Six months later the budget question still raged and Ridgway was just as adament: "The only alternative is to effect savings of dollars by expendature of lives."

Throughout the war, the Korean landscape presented logisticians with immense challenges. (**Above**) Men of the 23d Signal Battalion placing a 600-pair cable; (**below**) Marines of the 1st Shore Party Battalion building a concrete pipe bridge across a frigid river; and (**opposite**) Corporal Elmer Soprano of the 4th Signal Battalion rehabilitating the telephone lines along the Seoul-Pusan railroad near Chech'on.

If there is a lighter side to war, the American soldier will find it. Below are cartoons sent in to the Pacific Edition of the Army newspaper *Stars and Stripes* by men in the field.

"He's the best grenade thrower in the company."

"You seen our pack mule?"

"I don't care how accurate it is, get rid of it!"

"Well, sir, that depends. Just where is the stockade located?"

"Now I don't mind it if ya live here, but ya gotta stop bringin'
yer friends around fer them parties late at night!"

"Most amazing case, colonel. What stumps us
is how he removed his helmet."

"If they attack, I want you to make them **pay** for every inch of this hill!"

"Hey sarge, it must be spring— your sakura's bloomin'!"

"Talk about wires all fouled up— you know
anyone at Fairfax 2-1991, Kansas City, Kansas?"

"Sure ain't hard to spot the music lovers."

"Hello service battery? You better get hold of some ordinance people
and come on up here. Somebody's fouled up somewhere!"

"Hey, fellows! Look what Special Services gave us!"

With the suspension of all UN offensive operations in November of 1951, the thrust and counterthrust at the truce table became the only discernible maneuvers in what had become a self-imposed stalemate. (**Right**) Colonels James C. Murray, US Marine Corps, and Chang Chun San, NKPA, initial a map displaying a demarcation line between UN and Communist forces, Panmunjom, 26 November 1951. (**Below**) Communist negotiators at the original Keasong conference site, 16 July 1951. Former NKPA Chief of Staff, Lieutenant General Nam II (*center*), led the Communist delegation throughout the two years of armistice talks. The delegates to his right are from the CCF. (**Bottom**) Members of the UN negotiation team in a strategy session at their base camp in Munsan-ni, 5 March 1952. Vice Admiral C. Turner Joy, who headed the UN delegation, is at center with hands clasped. He was succeeded in command by Lieutenant General William K. Harrison in May. (**Opposite**) The negotiation site at Panmunjom as seen from an approaching helicopter and a meeting of the Military Armistice Conference.

The 155-mile front generally remained quiet during the opening days of 1952. Fighting was mostly confined to patrol clashes and raids which were designed to inflict the maximum amount of Communist casualties. (**Opposite top**) Soldiers of the newly-arrived 40th Infantry Division during a brief fire fight near Song Sil-li, Wednesday, 16 January; (**opposite bottom**) a squad moves out on a New Year's Day patrol from 2d Infantry Division bunker positions near Kumgangsan Tuesday, 1 January; and (**above**) Lieutenant Don S. Brimball of the 24th Infantry Division crouches behind the turret of his tank after giving the order to fire at the town of Song Sil-li, Thursday, 10 January.

Troops from an unidentified unit enjoying a New Year's celebration. The young boy in army fatigues is probably a war orphan that was "adopted" by the combat unit until he could be sent to one of the children's homes being organized in the rear areas by the ROK and church groups. Children whose parents and relatives had been killed in the fighting were often found living in the hills and shattered villages. (**Opposite bottom**) US soldiers and Katusas of the 2d Infantry Division prepare to go out on patrol under the leadership of Sergeant Elijah McLaughlin (*left*) and 2d Division troops (**opposite top**) scramble up the side of a steep hill as medic Presley J. Schmidt dresses a rifleman's leg wound, Thursday, 14 February 1952.

A memorial service is held in honor of the late King George VI of England at the headquarters of the British Commonwealth Division near the Imjin River, Wednesday, 6 February 1952. Officers and men from all sections of the division are led in prayer by Chaplain W. R. Rhys at an altar between the half-mast flags of Great Britain and the United Nations.

Soldiers of the Turkish Brigade keep a sharp lookout for movement along the barbed wire protecting their bunker on the main line of resistance (MLR), Monday, 14 April 1952.

A snowstorm blowing out of Manchuria doesn't stop the crew of this 155-mm. howitzer from pounding Communist troops on the central front, Thursday, 21 February 1952. (**Opposite top**) ROK 11th Division forward observers watch as phosphorus rounds explode on a nearby ridge, Monday, 17 March. (**Opposite bottom**) 2d Infantry Division tankers attached to the ROK 8th Division take cover behind a bank of earth as Chinese fire pins them down away from their armor, Friday, 25 April.

While still the undisputed masters of light infantry techniques, such as night movement and infiltration, the CCF showed that it was also adept at positional warfare. When the Eighth Army stabilized the front by calling a halt to its offensive operations, the Chinese built a series of heavily fortified defense lines based on a succession of ridges and hills running north as far as 15 miles from the line of contact. The CCF also began to receive large quantities of Soviet-made heavy artillery to replace the odd assortment of cannons they had, by now, moved into Korea. Chinese artillerymen quickly grew adept at massing fire on specific targets and displaced their guns with such frequency that US counterbattery efforts were rendered ineffective.

(**Top**) An artillery unit's forward observation post. (**Center**) Obsolescent 150-mm. Type 4 howitzers captured from the Japanese and (**bottom**) US 105-mm. M2A1 guns captured from the Nationalist Chinese. Large quantities of shells had also fallen into Communist hands and they apparently were able to manufacture at least some their own ordinance at captured munitions plants. (**Opposite**) Staged photographs of a CCF soldier throwing stick-mounted hand grenades and "US aggressors" surrendering during "the fiasco suffered by US imperialism's paper tigers in Korea."

A 7th Infantry Division rifleman fires at Communist soldiers on the next hill, Tuesday, 6 May 1952. (**Opposite top**) 2d Infantry Division Sherman firing in support of ROK troops near Kanmubong Ridge on the east central front, Sunday, 11 May. Note the sand bags piled on the tank's rear deck to protect its thinly armored engine compartment from the close-in fire of would-be infiltrators. (**Opposite bottom**) A 45th Infantry Division 4.2-inch mortar crew firing on Chinese forces in the Yokkok-ch'on River area west of Ch'orwon, Monday, 5 May. During that month, the division was on the receiving end of several large CCF raids which, in turn, precipitated the 45th pushing its outpost line forward by about a mile in June.

When the 132,000 prisoners of war in UN compounds were polled on whether or not they wished to return to Communism, only about one-third of the Chinese "volunteers" and half of the North Koreans said they were willing to go back. Roughly 40,000 South Koreans impressed into the NKPA had already been paroled. The Communist's displeasure over the UN practice of screening POWs soon exploded in a series of riots directed by special agents who, in some cases, allowed themselves to be captured so that they could infiltrate the prison camps. A half-dozen compounds at the Koje Island camp near Pusan were taken over by the Communists, the camp commandant was taken hostage and dozens of anti-communist prisoners were brutally murdered. In a final battle at the camp on Tuesday, 10 June 1952, the last compound was cleared by US paratroopers. One soldier was speared to death and 31 prisoners were killed, about a third by the Communists themselves. (**Above**) NKPA soldiers who expressed a desire to stay in South Korea and (**right**) prisoners marching out to be screened, 25 June. (**Opposite top**) A guard's-eye view of one of Koje's 30 compounds and (**opposite bottom**) die-hard Communist POWs drilling with spears and clubs fashioned from tent poles in a seized compound, Friday, 30 May.

A 105-mm. gun crew of Battery B, 37th Field Artillery Battalion supporting the 2d Infantry Division's battle for Old Baldy on Tuesday, 22 July 1952, and (**below**) a 155-mm. rifle of the 780th Field Artillery Battalion firing in support of 25th Infantry Division operations in the Mungdung-ni Valley, Thursday, 7 August.

In a scene made familiar to Americans through the opening credits of thousands of *M*A*S*H* television reruns, a soldier looks skyward as a Bell H-13 Souix prepares to evacuate a wounded soldier from a mine field near Chip'yong-ni.

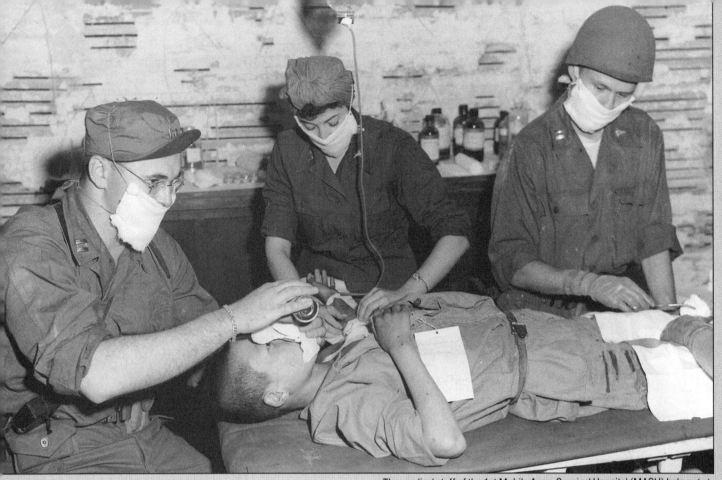

The medical staff of the 1st Mobile Army Surgical Hospital (MASH) help out at a civilian hospital in Inch'on, Tuesday, 3 October 1950. Treating the wounded Korean boy are (*left to right*) Captains John M. McGuire, Margaret C. Zane and Dexter T. Hall. (**Below**) Captains Arthur W. Adams and Anastasia E. Gianarakos performing a stomach operation at the 4th Field Hospital, Sunday, 6 January 1951. (**Opposite**) After trading in her combat boots for a comfortable pair of old shoes, Captain Jane Thurness puts her helmet to good use as a wash basin. Unlike the rather well-appointed tent of the television character "Hot Lips" Houlihan, the combination night stand and bureau to her right contains the few small luxuries Captain Thurness posesses in the tent she calls home.

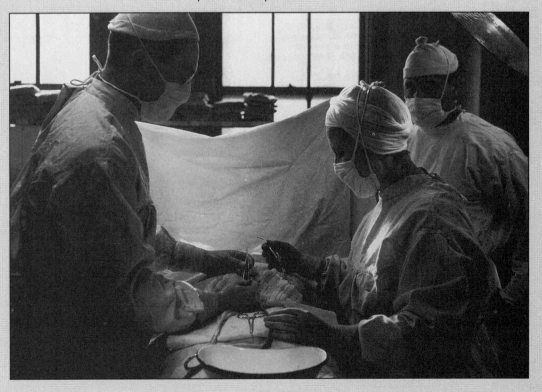

(**Opposite top**) The most fought over piece of real estate during the Korean War: the battered slopes of Old Baldy. Troops of the 2d Infantry Division can be seen along the skyline at left on Monday, 22 September 1952, the day after a successful counterattack regained the hill. Also, barely visible along the skyline are about a half-dozen bunkers. (**Opposite bottom**) A quad-50 adds its murderous fire power to the Sunday counterattack which dislodged the Chinese. (**Left**) Sergeant P. Weiner of the 2d Division (*foreground*) takes a break during a lull in the fighting, Friday, 1 August. (**Below**) Across the peninsula, a Sherman tank blasts Communist bunkers north of the Punchbowl, Monday, 1 September.

British Commonwealth Division artillerymen, manhandling a 25-pounder field gun near the Imjin River, and (**below**) mortarmen supporting 3d Infantry Division operations west of Yonch'on, September 1952. Left to right in the forward observation post: Sergeant William F. Loos of the 3d Division, Gunner Roy Martin, Captain Tony Ayling and Gunner John Croft. The 3d lost 350 men that month in an unsuccessful attempt to retain Outpost Kelley west of the Imjin River. (**Opposite**) 7th Infantry Division troops move cautiously along a shallow trench in the Iron Triangle. The 7th was engaged in a costly series of inconclusive actions during October and the first half of November.

Lieutenant Jerry King of the 3d Infantry Division relaxes with a letter from home after returning from six days of duty at an outpost beyond the main line of resistance, Sunday, 2 December 1952. (**Below**) A Patton tank pinch-hits as a mail truck as it moves to the front, Friday, 7 December 1951.

(**Left**) A happy, tattooed member of the 1st Marine Division wears one of the first armored vests to reach Korea in 1952. Although the vests would generally not stop bullets, they significantly lowered combat deaths and injuries by providing excellent protection against grenade, mortar and artillery fragments. (**Above**) A leatherneck clad in the new body armor walks away from an abandoned hut after setting it afire with a phosporous grenade to prevent its use by enemy snipers. Similar images from a later war would elicit howls of protest from peace groups.

During a light snowfall, Marines advance against an objective on the I Corps front with the support of Patton tanks, Friday, 12 December 1952. (**Below**) Captain Charles J. Kling, a 45th Infantry Division company commander, briefs Corporal Donald Walker and Private Edward C. Schaefer before they lead their patrol on a mission, Monday, 22 December.

Troops of the 3d Infantry Division enjoying their Thanksgiving dinner at a forward outpost near Ch'orwon. A week later on Thursday, 4 December 1952, the division played host to President-elect Dwight D. Eisenhower seen here with Sergeant Virgil Hutcherson, a squad leader.

(**Opposite**) A 2d Infantry Division M18 57-mm. recoilless rifle team
blasts Communist positions on New Year's Eve and, on New Year's Day, a
snow-suited 2d Division sniper hugs the ground on the left flank of a patrol
he is covering. (**Above**) A platoon's freshly scrubbed laundry is caught by a
sudden snowfall while still on a telephone wire clothesline.

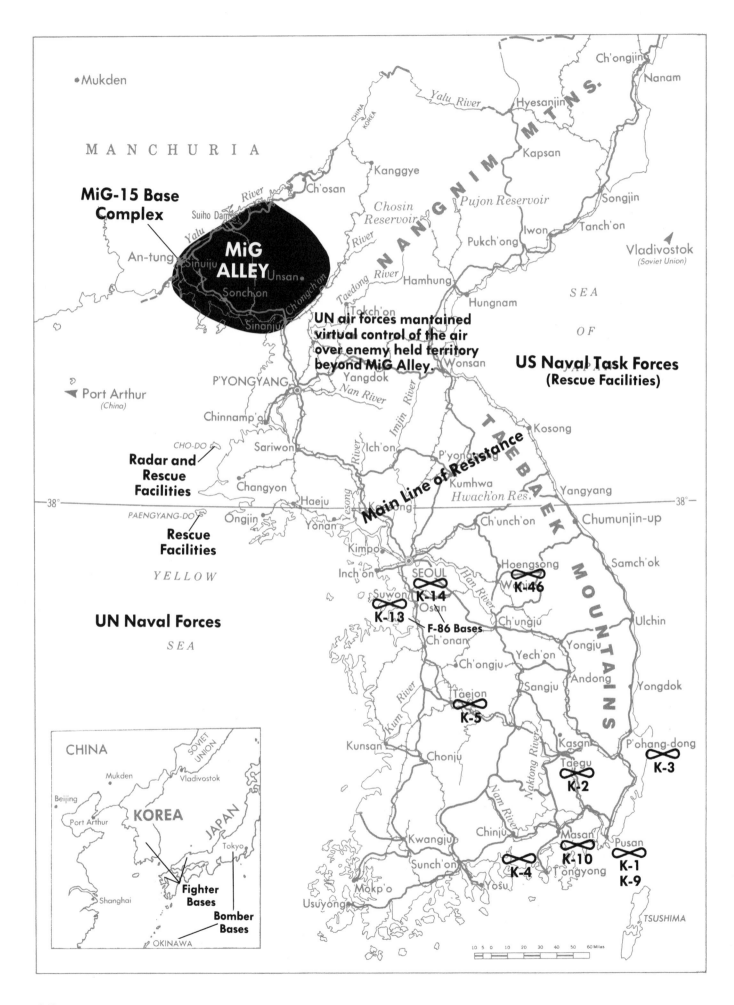

MiG-15 Base Complex

MANCHURIA

•Mukden

MiG ALLEY

An-tung

Suiho Dam

Ch'osan

Yalu River

Kanggye

Chosin Reservoir

Pujon Reservoir

Ch'ongjin

Nanam

Hyesanjin

Kapsan

Songjin

N A N G N I M   M T N S.

Iwon

Tanch'on

Pukch'ong

Sinuiju

Unsan

Sonch'on

Sinanju

Taedong River

Chongch'on River

Tokch'on

Hamhung

Hungnam

UN air forces mantained virtual control of the air over enemy held territory beyond MiG Alley.

Wonsan

SEA

OF

Vladivostok
(Soviet Union)

◄ Port Arthur
(China)

P'YONGYANG

Yangdok

Nan River

Imjin River

US Naval Task Forces
(Rescue Facilities)

Chinnamp'o

Kosong

CHO-DO

Radar and Rescue Facilities

Sariwon

Changyon

Ryesong River

Ich'on

P'yonggang

Kumhwa
Hwach'on Res.

Main Line of Resistance

Yangyang

T A E B A E K   M O U N T A I N S

—38°

PAENGYANG-DO

Haeju

Ongjin

Yonan

Ch'unch'on

Chumunjin-up

—38°

Rescue Facilities

YELLOW

Kimpo

Inch'on

SEOUL

Suwon

K-14

Osan

Hoengsong
Wonju

K-46

Samch'ok

UN Naval Forces

SEA

K-13

F-86 Bases

Ch'onan

Han River

Ch'ungju

Ulchin

Ch'ongju

Yech'on

Yongju

Andong

Kum River

Taejon

K-5

Sangju

Yongdok

Kunsan

Chonju

Naktong River

Kasan

Taegu

P'ohang-dong

K-3

K-2

Kwangju

Chinju

Nam River

Masan

K-10

Pusan

K-1
K-9

Sunch'on

K-4

T'ongyong

Mokp'o

Yosu

Usuyonge

TSUSHIMA

Inset map:

CHINA

SOVIET UNION

Mukden

Vladivostok

Beijing

KOREA

JAPAN

Port Arthur

Tokyo

Fighter Bases

Shanghai

Bomber Bases

OKINAWA

10 5 0   10   20   30   40   50   60 Miles

CHAPTER EIGHT

The Air War

At high noon on Tuesday, 27 June 1950, the first shoot out between US and Communist pilots occurred 10,000 ft. above the streets of Seoul. US nationals were being evacuated from the capital's Kimpo Airport and a Military Air Transport Service C-54 had been destroyed on the ground the day before, along with seven ROK training aircraft— nearly half of South Korea's tiny airforce. To prevent a repeat performance, relays of combat air patrols belonging to Lieutenant General George E. Stratemeyer's Far East Air Force were sent from Japan to protect the helpless transports. Five F-82 Twin Mustang all-weather fighters circling high over the capital spotted seven Yak-3 fighters heading toward Kimpo and immediately engaged them; downing three for no losses. After another uneven dogfight in the early afternoon saw all four marauding Il-10 *Shturmovik* fighter bombers shot down by an equal number of F-80 Shooting Stars, the North Koreans refrained from sending more aircraft to certain destruction in the Seoul-Kimpo area.

The Far East Air Force (FEAF) in 1950 was a potent fighting force in spite of postwar strength reductions in its air units. The heart of the FEAF was located in an airfield complex near Tokyo but, in the hectic opening days of the conflict, it was able to immediately draw upon reserves from major bases to the south on Okinawa and the Philippine Islands and to the east on Guam. In Japan itself, bases were spread from Itazuke on the southern island of Kyushu through Misawa on the northeast coast of Honshu. A squadron of Australian F-51 Mustangs* at southern Honshu's Iwakuni airfield, near the Korean battleground, was also made available on June 30. By the end of July, the FEAF had flown 57 sorties in two strategic bombing strikes,

4,300 in close support of ground troops, 2,550 interdicting Communist supply lines and 1,600 less glamorous but vital reconnaissance and supply missions.

Unfortunately, the FEAF was having to work with aircraft not entirely suited to the war being fought. The new F-84 Thunderstreak was specially adapted to air-ground operations but required runways much longer than those available in Japan. The FEAF commander desperately wanted more all-weather Twin Mustangs but, for strategic reasons, they had to be retained for the defense of Alaska and the Pacific Northwest. Likewise, the B-36 and all-jet B-47 remained part of the strategic reserve in case Korea turned out to be the prelude to a larger war. Only the venerable B-29 Superfortress, now downgraded from a "heavy" to a "medium" bomber, would see action and even its upgraded B-50 version couldn't be released for Far East service.

The two fighters the FEAF used for the immediate task at hand— supporting the combat troops on the ground— were not designed for such missions. The Shooting Star was a fuel-guzzling, counter-air interceptor. When loaded with the little ordnance it could carry and given extra fuel tanks to make the round trip from Japan, its operational range was so shortened that it could spend little or no time over the target to coordinate its attack. Huge numbers of propeller-driven Mustangs were readily available from stocks in the United States but, as combat operations in the

---

*In June 1948, the Pursuit (P) designation used for certain US Air Force aircraft types was changed to Fighter (F). Hence, the Mustang, which had become famous as the P-51 during World War II, was now called the F-51. Attack (A) designations were changed to Bomber (B). This resulted in the widely-used B-26 of the Korean War— built by Douglas and called the Invader— being a completely different aircraft than the discontinued B-26 of the previous war which was built by Martin and called the Marauder.

The crew of a 3d Bomb Group B-26 Invader make final preparations for a night mission against Communist supply routes, June 1951.

Second World War had amply demonstrated, its vulnerable liquid coolant lines and radiator made it highly susceptible to antiaircraft and small arms fire. The US Navy still utilized rugged, air-cooled, radial engines on their Corsairs and Skyraiders but a similar Air Force plane, the F-47 Thunderbolt, was no longer in production and too few were available to be employed in Korea.

In spite of the severe operational limitations of its aircraft, the FEAF performed superbly with what it had. The tough little Mustangs staged strikes from airstrips at Taegu and, until they were forced out, from P'ohang-dong; and a partial solution was found to the Shooting Star's range problem. The jet's two supplementary fuel tanks were replaced with larger jury-rigged tanks giving the F-80s 200 more gallons of fuel and approximately one hour more flight time at full load. The huge wing tanks were put into production in Japan and General Stratemeyer lobbied hard to obtain every Shooting Star he could get his hands on.

The successful invasion at Inch'on and rapid drive to the Yalu River allowed the FEAF to base substantial numbers of aircraft in Korea itself. The Chinese counterstroke in the winter of 1950 never seriously threatened to overrun the southernmost FEAF bases, although Kimpo and nearby Suwon were abandoned and a huge store of aviation fuel had to be destroyed. A greater threat came from the appearance of the Soviet-built MiG-15 jet fighter in Korean skies.

The onset of the first Chinese offensive in November 1950 brought the chunky-looking jets streaking down from their base at An-tung and only the inexperience of the Chinese pilots— plus the relatively low number of MiGs employed— prevented disaster. The MiG-15 completely outclassed every friendly aircraft in the war zone and the US Air Force scrambled to get the 4th Fighter-Interceptor Wing's high-performance F-86 Sabre jets to the Far East theater from their base at the New Castle County Airport in Wilmington, Delaware. MiGs and Sabres first tangled on Sunday, 17 December, when a MiG was shot down in flames near the Yalu. The dogfights grew in size and intensity over northwest Korea's MiG Alley with the Sabre pilots racking up large numbers of kills in spite of their prohibition from engaging in "hot pursuit" of MiGs escaping to Chinese territory.

But while the number of operational Sabre squadrons remained fixed at two, the number of MiGs made available to the Chinese Communists grew steadily. It soon became apparent that there simply were not enough Sabres to protect the slower aircraft conducting the bomber campaigns. B-29s, F-80s and the newly-committed F-84s were being shot down in increasing numbers and the depredations of the Chinese pilots forced the FEAF's Superfortresses to abandon daylight precision bombing in October 1951.

Night bombing by short-range navigation radar

(SHORAN) proved highly effective in strikes against the North Korean airfields the Communists were trying to put into working order; but the enemy's growing number of aircraft and ability to quickly repair damaged runways added up to a bleak future for UN air superiority. Persistent warnings by FEAF vice-commander Major General Otto P. Weyland that "there is a definite possibility that the enemy will be able to establish (MiG) bases in Korea and threaten our supremacy over the front" were now acted on. In December, a squadron of Sabres was brought over from Japan and the 51st Fighter-Interceptor Wing's two F-80 squadrons were traded in for F-86s. The FEAF now had five Sabre squadrons in Korea and UN air superiority was never again in doubt. Confirmed Communist losses would eventually total 1108 planes, 838 of them MiGs, against a total UN loss of 114 aircraft in air-to-air combat.

Ostensibly less effective than the effort to neutralize North Korean airfields and retain air supremacy was the battle to stop the flow of Communist supplies to the front. The first in a series of road and rail interdiction campaigns continued at a fever pitch throughout the summer and fall of 1951 but the results did not live up to expectations engendered by its name, STRANGLE. North Korean laborers always seemed able to repair tracks and bridges as fast as FEAF and naval aircraft chopped them up, and much criticism was leveled at air planners. In hindsight, though, it is clear that while the Communists' supply system was never destroyed, only enough material got through to carry on a static defense while maintaining a slow, incremental build-up. Even after two full years of stockpiling, the Chinese still had great difficulty maintaining their 1953 offensive.

In addition to the daily grind of air superiority, ground support, supply interdiction and reconnaissance missions, there were numerous FEAF efforts to support the negotiation process at Panmunjon by putting direct pressure on the Communists. Ridgway's replacment as Far East and UN commander, General Mark W. Clark, looked back at the year of futile negotiations and stated his belief that "only through forceful action could the Communists be made to agree to an armistice the United States considered honorable." Clark asked his air, naval and ground force commanders what he could do to "make the Communists realize that the price of peace is not as cheap as they are trying to make it." General Weyland, who had recently been promoted to commander in chief of FEAF, suggested that attacking North Korea's hydroelectric power system would fit the bill.

The key power facilities at Fusen, Suiho, Chosin and Kyosen had been targeted for destruction as early as September of 1950. A Joint Chiefs of Staff study estimated that the loss of electricity from the system "would be a severe economic blow to Manchuria" and both the State and Defense Departments believed that to attack them would risk widening the war. By the summer of 1952, the weight of high-level opinion had swung to the side of those who believed that a more aggressive air campaign would demonstrate to the Communists that their continued prosecution of the war would only increase in cost, yet not change the conflict's limited nature.

The North Korean power system was destroyed in a series of massive, well-coordinated attacks by land and carrier-based aircraft from 23 to 27 June. Scarce Soviet and Chinese technicians were sent to the peninsula to repair the damage but, after a two-week blackout, only partial service was restored and continued attacks by UN aircraft ensured that, as long as hostilities continued, power would not rise above 10 percent of its former output. As expected, key Chinese industrial areas in Manchuria were essentially shut down and the province fell 23 percent short of its electrical requirements for the year, making it impossible to fill Beijing's production quotas. Industrial and military targets in P'yongyang were also hit for the first time in August and, after three all-out strikes, there were no more "worthwile targets" in the capital.

The pressure was maintained in spite of loud international condemnation— especially in Great Britain— and increased when the Communists bitterly rejected another set of UN cease-fire proposals in May 1953. FEAF intelligence officers had long argued that a *growing* rice crop was just as legitimate a target as a warehouse of harvested rice and, in an effort to encourage the Communists to more carefully consider the UN position, General Clark ordered the Toksan and Chasan irrigation dams destroyed. The attacks, on 13 and 15 May, and the North Korean's own countermeasures at other dams, halved rice production and the resulting floods did more damage to the rail lines into P'yongyang than months of interdiction bombing. As the war neared an end, North Korea was clearly reeling from the FEAF's hammer blows and even Manchuria was suffering.

On 22 May 1953, Secretary of State John Foster Dulles visited India's Prime Minister, Jawaharlal Nehru. Dulles took the opportunity to mention to his host that the United States had decided to attack Communist bases in their Manchurian sanctuary if the deadlock in negotiations continued. Knowing that the Indian and Red Chinese governments kept in close consultation on a wide variety of matters and the Chinese had used India as a conduit for their warnings to the United Nations, Dulles believed that the Indian government would transmit his threat as well. Apparently it did and key sticking points in the armistice terms were worked out to the UN's satisfaction with unusual speed.

The ability of the venerable F-51 Mustang to operate close to the front under very austere conditiions made it the FEAFs most reliable asset at the beginning of the war. (**Opposite**) Crew chief Lance Corporal Bob Bell, sweats out the return of Royal Australian Air Force F-51s to their base at Iwakuni, Japan on Tuesday, 18 July 1950. Mustangs from Japan were regularly staged through advance air strips within the Pusan Perimeter during the summer battles. (**Above**) US and South African F-51 fighters being refueled and rearmed at P'yongyang's East Airfield, late November 1950. (**Below**) A US Air Force F-51 plows through monsoon waters.

"Truck Hunters" of the 35th Fighter Interceptor Group and its attached Royal Australian Air Force squadron are debriefed following a mass air strike in the Chip'yong-ni area southeast of Seoul, mid-February 1951. During the Communist's offensive along the Wonju-Hoengsong axis, the enemy was so desperate to move supplies forward that they even kept their trucks rolling in daylight hours. In the resultant feast, Fifth Air Force Mustangs consumed 236 trucks and damaged 83 more at the height of the offensive on Tuesday, 13 February. F-80 Shooting Stars destroyed 40 additional vehicles that day.

The screaming whine and speed of the F-80 Shooting Star's attack greatly affected NKPA troop morale. Initially, the fuel-guzzling jets were unable to spend much time over target areas but the addition of two massive, 265-gallon fuel tanks to each aircraft helped rectify the problem. The US Air Force Material Command refused to approve the installation of the jury-rigged tanks, because of the severe stress they placed on the F-80's wing tips and shackles, but was overridden by the FEAF because of the ground troops' critical need for air support. The "Misawa tanks" were put into mass production at a Japanese factory and the Shooting Star's designer, Kelley Johnson, soon came to Korea to see for himself what was going on. The first time he watched his delicate, counter-air interceptor take off with the fully loaded tanks plus a 500-pound bomb, he turned away with a anguished look on his face and said, "I can't watch it."

Armed with no less than 14 forward-firing .50-caliber machineguns and up to 4,000 pounds of bombs or rockets, B-26 Invader light bombers were committed to battle within hours of President Truman's authorization to provide the Republic of Korea with air support. Thirty-seven months later they dropped the last bombs of the war a half-hour before the cease fire took effect. The B-26 was heavily armored to afford protection against ground fire and use of radar permitted it to make highly effective bombing attacks by night. From the beginning of 1951 onwards, the Invader was almost totally engaged in this type of opereation. (**Above**) Trains and rail facilities between P'yongyang and Wonsan being put to the napalm torch by B-26 bombers, April 1953. (**Opposite top**) An Invader drops canisters filled with propaganda leaflets, November 1952, and Lieutenant David O. Stegal, wounded during a night mission, is helped down by Lieutenants Charles M. Coin (*left*) and Henry Van DePol, the base surgeon, at Iwakuni Field, Japan, on Tuesday, 18 July 1950. (**Opposite bottom**) Napalm bombs exploding among Communist barracks west of Chongsoktu-ri, Friday, 2 February 1951. A B-26 can be seen at upper left.

UN air superiority allowed light aircraft to enjoy unfettered access to the skys over battle areas when engaged in reconnaissance and artillery spotting. But while such aircraft did not have to worry about marauding Communist fighters, the photo above of a shot-up T-6 tail assembly makes it clear that enemy ground forces did their best to make the spotters feel unwelcome. (**Opposite**) Private Donald Hildreth demonstrating the use of a K-20 camera from the rear seat of an L-5 aircraft and a 3d Infantry Division L-19 during an observation flight over the western front.

Two light-case, 500-pound napalm bombs a split second after their release from an F-51 Mustang over a North Korean industrial target. The bomb closest to the camera plummets nose first while the other still retains its horizontal position. (**Opposite**) The destructive capacity of a napalm bomb can be seen in this Fifth Air Force test on a captured T-34 tank. The 100-pound bomb created a pear-shaped, 1,500-degree explosion which incinerated an area roughly 275 feet long by 80 feet wide.

Napalm was extremely effective against vehicles of all types— including T34 tanks whose rubber-rimmed wheels would ignite even from a near miss. As a practical matter, though, the Air Force believed that fragmentation bombs were a more efficient infantry-killer but felt that use of napalm was better for our own troop's morale and was certainly demoralizing to NKPA foot soldiers. The commander of the first detachment of F-51s to operate out of a Korean airstrip during the 1950 invasion of South Korea, Major Dean E. Hess, observed that: "The enemy didn't seem to mind being blown up or shot. However, as soon as we would start dropping thermite or napalm in their vicinity they would immediately scatter and break any forward movement." Later that year, during the winter battles near the Chosin Reservoir, Marines would be amused to see Chinese troops hurry to the sites of still-burning napalm strikes to warm themselves against the sub-zero cold.

Although some operations would utilize anywhere from 40 to nearly a hundred B-29 Superfortresses, the nature of the targets in Korea dictated that raids be conducted by much smaller groups of 8 or 9 aircraft. Thirteen of the medium bombers were either shot down or severely damaged during the last week of October 1951 prompting the suspension of daylight precision bombing in favor of night bombing by radar. Most of the losses were from MiG-15 jet fighters based in China. (**Top**) A B-29 returning to its base on Okinawa, October 1951, and (**above**) engine mechanics and technicians swarming over a B-29 in Japan are shielded from the broiling sun by canopies, September 1952. (**Opposite**) B-29s raining tons of bombs on a North Korean target in January 1951 and Wonsan's railroad repair yard before and during a Thursday, 10 August 1950 bomb run.

265

By the summer of 1951, Chinese MiG-15 jet fighters were streaming down from their An-tung base complex in "trains" of 90 or more aircraft. Pitched battles erupted in northwest Korea's "MiG Alley" throughout the fall and winter as US F-86 Sabre jets struggled to retain control of the air war. Timely reinforcements, exceptional pilot training and tactics— plus an aggressive policy of not allowing the Communists to rebuild their North Korean air bases— forced the Chinese to scale back their air effort and from 1952 on they appeared to use Korea only as a training and testing ground. (**Opposite**) F-86 gun camera film of a MiG pilot being propelled from his crippled plane after firing an ejection charge and close-up photos of a brand-new MiG-15bis (Encore) being flight tested by a US pilot after it was flown to Japan by a defector. (**Above**) F-86F Sabres of the FEAF. MiG-15s were generally faster, more maneuverable and had a better rate of climb than Sabres at altitudes over 35,000 feet but were unstable, had a nasty tendency to stall out at low speeds and snap into uncontrollable spins during evasion maneuvers. MiG-15s were armed with two 23-mm. and one slow-firing 37-mm. cannons while Sabres fired six .50-caliber machine guns.

(**Opposite**) Sabres of the 51st Fighter Interceptor Wing patroling "MiG Alley," between the Yalu and Ch'ongch'on Rivers, in October 1952. The previous month, four Sabres were lost while knocking down 61 to 68 MiG-15s and damaging at least 57 others. By the end of the war, only 78 Sabres had been destroyed in air battles which had cost the Chinese a minimum of 792 MiG-15s. (**Above**) Dozens of streamlined gasoline drop tanks are unloaded by Korean laborers at Kimpo Air Base. The rapid deployment of additional Sabres to Korea at the end of 1951 outstripped stocks of the fuel tanks and for several months, pilots often flew into combat with only one attached to their aircraft. (**Left**) 300-degrees of searing air from a portable warming unit melts snow and warms up a Sabre engine prior to a December 1952 patrol.

The US Air Force utilized SA-16 Albatross flying boats and H-19 Chickasaw helicopters to pick up downed pilots on land or sea while the Navy used PBM-5 Mariner flying boats and HO3S-1 helicopters. The Air Force and Navy rescue aircraft were protected by combat air patrols of F-51 Mustangs and F4U Corsairs respectively. (**Above**) An H-19 helicopter low over the Han River near Seoul. (**Right**) Sergeant Basil L. Boatright of the 3d Air Rescue Squadron makes sure that the chopper pilots have no commuting worries— he rigged the alert tent next to the scene of operations, Friday, 6 April 1951. (**Opposite**) The object of the rescue squadrons' attentions, combat pilots bound for North Korean air space. A sign on an oriental *torii*, or gateway, directs these F-86 pilots to where they might find some Soviet-built aircraft.

270

The F-86F was found to be an excellent platform for the delivery of ordinance on ground targets and FEAF pilots flying Mustangs made the difficult conversion to Sabres between November 1952 and February 1953. (**Above**) an F-86F peels into a screaming dive over a troop and supply center. Seconds after this photo was taken, a storehouse exploded after the Sabre's bullets ripped into a hidden stock of ammunition. (**Opposite**) A stick of bombs from a B-29 Superfortress walks up the runway of Hungnam's Yongp'o airfield. Constant reconnaissance of North Korean airfields allowed the FEAF to wait until the Communists were nearly finished repairing their airstrips before sending the bombers on another mission to blast more "postholes" and keep the runways unusable.

On Thursday, 9 November, 1950, two of the first MiG-15s encountered by UN forces were shot down by carrier-based F9F Panthers. Over the next few years, however, the deployment of the Navy's large Essex class aircraft carriers off Korea's east coast— well away from MiG Alley— presented Panther pilots with few opportunities to get a crack at the Communist fighters. Meanwhile, British Commonwealth jet jockeys serving with the 77th Royal Australian Air Force Squadron flew straight-winged Meteor-8 interceptors which were badly outclassed by the swept-wing MiGs.

The few Marine and British Commonwealth pilots serving on exchange duty with the Air Force Sabre squadrons doing battle along the Yalu had the best chance of shooting down MiGs. (**Opposite**) Flight Lieutenant Henry Buttleman of West Mersea, Essex, England (*top, third from left*) walking out to the flight line with other Sabre pilots while a grinning leatherneck airman named John Glenn poses next to his Sabre suitably emblasoned with the legend "MIG MAD MARINE." In a little over a week, Major Glenn downed three of the Soviet-built jets but the signing of the Armistice cut short his hot streak. (**Above**) ROK Air Force pilots Captain Chun Hyung and Major Raik Hyun being briefed by US Sabre pilots. The South Koreans flew F-51 Mustangs throughout the war and did not convert over to F-86 jets until 1954.

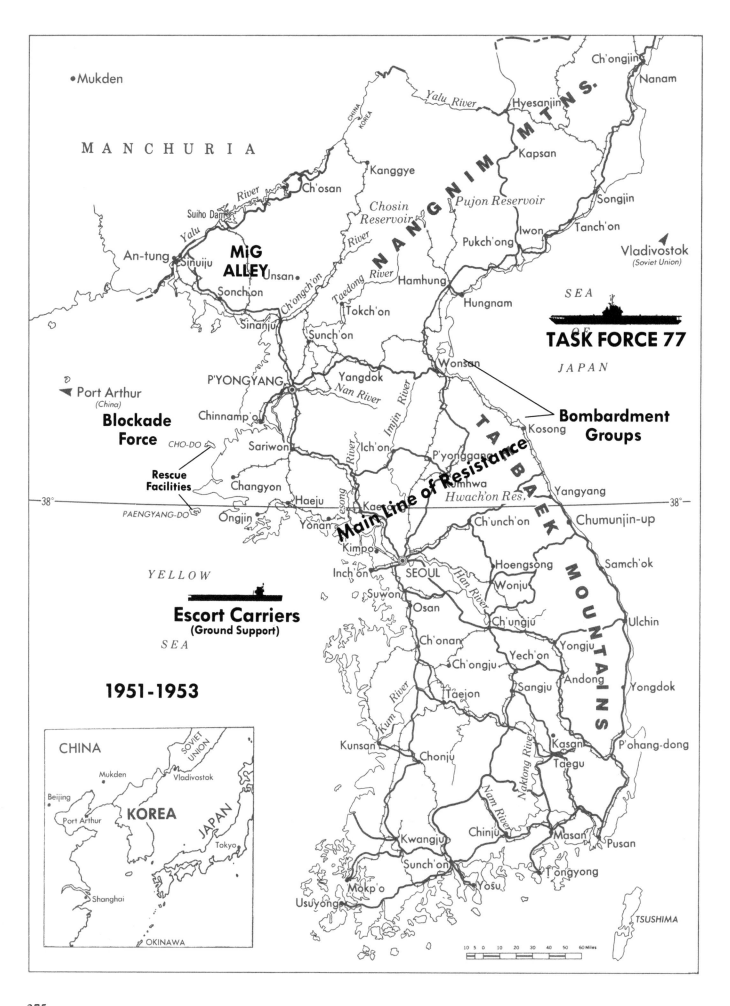

MANCHURIA

Mukden

Ch'ongjin

Nanam

Yalu River

HYESANJIN

Kapsan

Kanggye

Ch'osan

Songjin

Suiho Dam

Pujon Reservoir

Chosin Reservoir

An-tung

MiG ALLEY

Sinuiju

Unsan

Sonch'on

Iwon

Tanch'on

Pukch'ong

Vladivostok
(Soviet Union)

Sinanju

Tokch'on

Hamhung

Hungnam

Sunch'on

Ch'ongch'on River

Taedong River

SEA OF JAPAN

TASK FORCE 77

Port Arthur
(China)

Blockade Force

P'YONGYANG

Yangdok

Nan River

Wonsan

Bombardment Groups

CHO-DO

Chinnamp'o

Sariwon

Ich'on

Kosong

Rescue Facilities

Changyon

P'yonggang

38°

PAENGYANG-DO

Haeju

Kaes

Kumhwa

Hwach'on Res.

Yangyang

38°

Ongjin

Yonan

Main Line of Resistance

Ch'unch'on

Chumunjin-up

Kimpo

Hoengsong

Samch'ok

Inch'on

SEOUL

Wonju

YELLOW

Suwon

Han River

Ulchin

Escort Carriers
(Ground Support)

Osan

Ch'ungju

SEA

Ch'onan

Yech'on

Yongju

Yongdok

1951-1953

Ch'ongju

Sangju

Andong

Taejon

Kum River

Naktong River

Kasan

Kunsan

Chonju

Taegu

P'ohang-dong

Nam River

Kwangju

Chinju

Masan

Pusan

Sunch'on

Tongyong

Mokp'o

Usuyong

Yosu

TSUSHIMA

10 5 0   10   20   30   40   50   60 Miles

CHINA

Mukden

SOVIET UNION

Vladivostok

Beijing

Port Arthur

KOREA

JAPAN

Tokyo

Shanghai

OKINAWA

CHAPTER NINE

The War at Sea

The opening of hostilities on the Korean peninsula found only two UN aircraft carriers in the Far East and, indeed, the entire western Pacific; the large, Essex class carrier, USS *Valley Forge* and smaller, British flattop, HMS *Triumph*. These ships, along with their escorting cruisers and destroyers, rendezvoused at Okinawa's Buckner Bay to form Task Force 77 on Tuesday, 27 June 1950. After a brief wait to see if the activity in Korea was only a prelude to an attack on Japan, the Commander, Naval Forces, Far East (COMNAVFE), Vice Admiral C. Turner Joy, ordered the task force to strike targets around the North Korean capital of P'yongyang. On Sunday, 1 July, TF 77 sailed north into the Yellow Sea. The *Triumph* launched 12 Fireflies and 9 Seafires against an airfield at Haeju while 12 Skyraiders, 8 Corsairs and 8 Panther jets sortied from the *Valley Forge* to hit the airfield outside P'yongyang. Eleven Yak fighters were shot down or strafed on the runways and additional strikes destroyed fuel tanks, a railroad bridge and 15 locomotives.

No UN aircraft were lost during the attacks but the carriers subsequently got their first taste of a problem that would plague operations throughout the war. A deck accident on the *Valley Forge* wrecked three planes and damaged six others when a shot-up Skyraider lost control of its wing flaps and was forced to make a "hot" landing. The stricken aircraft bounced over a crash barrier on the flight deck then plowed into the planes bunched together on the bow. Such accidents had always been a problem, but the advent of high-speed jets coupled with the lack of angled flight decks (which allow freshly landed aircraft to scoot out of the way of those coming in behind them) made large numbers of these mishaps inevitable on the World War II-era carriers. In fact, one of the two Panther squadrons on the *Valley Forge* received only a single bullet hole from enemy fire during its first two months off Korea yet logged no fewer than 35 crash landings.

The *Philippine Sea* added its air wing to the fray at the beginning of August while a sister ship, the *Boxer*, prepared for war at San Francisco's naval yard and the British *Theseus* received orders to join the growing UN fleet half a world away. The appearance of *Philippine Sea* was followed almost immediately by the arrival of the much smaller escort carri-

ers, *Badoeng Strait* and *Sicily*; giving the COMNAVFE a total of five carriers in Korean waters with another two on the way. Although each of these ships would perform a multitude of tasks, a simple division of labor was quickly established. The big boys on the block were the two 80-plane, Essex class carriers of TF 77. The *Philippine Sea* concentrated on trying to stop the flow of men and supplies down Korea's transportation arteries, while the *Valley Forge* and escort carriers of TF 96.8 (later TF 90.5) performed close air support missions. The *Triumph*, meanwhile, formed the core of TF 91 and worked hard to enforce a blockade of the Korean coast. Over a dozen more aircraft carriers would be rotated through the Far East theater by war's end.

The sea blockade was of particular importance because the Koreans had historically used their coastal waters to make up for the lack of an adequate transportation system in the interior. A huge fleet of boats and small ships had developed over the years and UN forces prevented the Communists from continuing to use them as they had along the peninsula's eastern seaboard at the beginning of the invasion when the North Koreans made a quick succession of amphibious landings at Kangnung, Shamch'ok, Ulchin and Yongdok. An attempted fifth landing at Chumunjin-up was foiled when a convoy and its torpedo boat escorts were intercepted by a British-American blockade group centered around the lightly armed but extremely fast anti-aircraft cruiser USS *Juneau*. Nine of the 14 North Korean vessels were sunk by naval gunfire on Sunday, 2 July 1950. The close blockade of enemy harbors and sea movement would last three years and be the longest operation of this type that the US Navy had been involved in since the Civil War.

Except for the brief period when it was in UN hands, the east coast port of Wonsan was struck almost daily by shells ranging in size from the 5- to 8-inch rounds fired from cruisers and destroyers to the mammoth 16-inch (406mm) projectiles blasted from the battleships *Missouri, Iowa, Wisconsin* and *New Jersey*. Up to three bombardment groups were simultaneously active in the Sea of Japan. A TF centered around cruisers, such as the *Helena, Manchester* and *St. Paul*, provided fire support for ROK units on the eastern end of the front while another kept up the punishment on

Wonsan. One or two battleships would add their weight to these missions and often range as far north as Ch'ongjin, near the Soviet border, striking harbors, the coastal rail line and other facilities. Shallow waters and the makeup of Korea's Yellow Sea coast generally precluded the use of deep-draft warships in the west but the *Missouri* did take part in the invasion at Inch'on.

Unlike World War II, where the Navy fought maritime-oriented campaigns across broad expanses of ocean, the nature of the war in Korea required that it be tied to a land campaign. The Red Chinese had no significant naval forces and the huge Soviet submarine fleet flanking Korea at Vladivostok in the east and Port Arthur on China's Liaotung Peninsula in the west remained nothing more than a menacing presence. Although numerous Soviet military aircraft probing the fleet's defenses did have to be intercepted and shot down, * the meat and potatoes of service in Korean waters consisted of providing gunfire and close air support for the hard-pressed troops ashore, the interdiction of Communist supply lines and, during the first six months, the execution of over a dozen evacuations and landings.

Throughout the war's first year, the close air support provided by Navy and Marine pilots saved countless UN lives on the battlefields below. As the fighting entered a more static phase in the summer of 1951, naval air assets were increasingly shifted to stopping the flow of supplies to the front. Carrier-based F4U Corsairs and AD-1 Skyraiders could be armed with roughly triple the ordnance of their Air Force counterparts and were able to haul the heavy payloads over longer distances. The limited range of FEAF interceptors also necessitated that the carrier's F9F Panther and new F2H Banshee jets escort the slow-moving B-29 bombers on their mission deep into the northern reaches of the country.

Carrier aircraft had completely destroyed the important oil refinery at Wonsan early in the war and were increasingly given special missions to perform. Torpedo-armed Skyraiders from the *Princeton* burst a dam at Hwach'on and, because the less maneuverable B-29s could easily stray into Soviet or Chinese airspace, targets near or *on* the border— such as the Yalu bridges and Suiho dam— were generally turned over to the Navy.

One unusual raid took place on the morning of Tuesday, 30 October 1951, when aircraft from the *Essex* and *Antietam* struck a large conference of Communist Party military and political leaders at Kapsan near the Manchurian border. Anti-Communist guerrillas in North Korea had gotten wind of the meeting and promptly notified Eighth Army intelligence which, in turn, passed it on to the Navy. Over 500 high-ranking Communists were killed and all of the North Korean Communist Party records were destroyed. The pilots of the eight Skyraiders that led the attack took

the names of Walt Disney's seven dwarfs for their call signs but Radio P'yongyang branded them "the butchers of Kapsan." Their leader, not surprisingly, went by the name Snow White.

Special missions were not limited to the Navy's air arm. On another occasion, The wreckage of a downed Soviet-built MiG-15 jet fighter was spotted under 17 feet of water on a sandbar 30 miles north of the Tae-dong Estuary. Despite the fact that superior pilot training enabled Navy pilots to come out on top in most encounters with the faster, high-flying MiGs, the recovery of this relatively intact aircraft would be a prize of inestimable intelligence value. From the new COMNAVFE, Vice Admiral Robert P. Biscoe, down to the lowliest seaman involved in the recovery operation, all were determined to snatch the jet.

On Friday, 20 July 1951, the Landing Ship Dock (LSD) USS *Whetstone* disgorged a crane-equipped Landing Ship Utility (LSU) whose crew worked feverishly for two days to free the submerged MiG from the imprisoning muck. The worksite was only a 10 minute flight from the Chinese airbase complex at An-tung but investigating MiGs were kept at a distance by bad weather and combat air patrols from the HMS *Glory* and USS *Sicily*, while the cruiser HMS *Belfast* and frigate HMS *Cardigan Bay* stood by to provide antiaircraft protection. After extracting everything of value from the hulk below, the LSU docked safely with the LSD USS *Epping Forest* and the MiG parts were flown to the United States for detailed analysis.

Major joint air strikes with the FEAF were conducted against North Korea's hydroelectric and transportation systems during the war's last years and and the dangerous MiGs began to take a toll of both land- and carrier-based aircraft. A Sea Fury from the HMS *Ocean* and a Corsair from the *Sicily* downed a MiG apiece but the propeller-driven fighters were obviously at a great disadvantage in dogfights with the Communist jets and were generally trading the Chinese plane-for-plane— an extremely high loss rate. The Navy's jets fared better, however. One serious scuffle broke out on Tuesday, 18 November 1952, as TF 77 supported a bombardment group operating near the Soviet border. Three Panthers intercepted seven Soviet MiGs streaking towards the carriers *Oriskany* and *Kearsarge* from Vladivostok, only 100 miles away. One Navy jet was badly shot up but the MiGs broke contact after two were downed and another so heavily damaged that it was probably lost.

The Navy and Marines lost 1,248 aircraft during the three years of war. Well over half were due to deck accidents and 564, including eight rescue helicopters, were destroyed by enemy action. MiGs accounted for only five losses with the balance downed by hostile ground fire. Four British, one Australian and seventeen American flattops served in the theater of operations and launched over 280,000 combat sorties; fully a third of all UN air missions. Aircraft carriers, which many argued would have only limited utility in a future, push-button war, had proved their worth in Korea.

---

* A Tu-2 light bomber on 4 September 1950 and three to five MiG-15 fighters on 18 November 1952.

An F4U Corsair of Air Group 11 catapults off the USS *Philippine Sea's* bow on its way to strike North Korean forces advancing on the Pusan Perimeter, Friday, 4 August 1950. Three days earlier, the *Philippine Sea* had joined the carriers HMS *Triumph* and USS *Valley Forge* whose air groups had been engaged in combat since the beginning of July.

With the day's flight operations concluded, crewmen pause by a Corsair on the hanger deck of the USS *Antietam* as the ship secures "flight quarters" and turns her attentions to the morrow's work, October, 1951. (**Opposite**) An F9F Panther from the USS *Bon Homme Richard* begins to pull up after dropping two 250-pound bombs (*see arrows*) and firing a 5-inch high-velocity rocket, November, 1952. This attack against a small highway bridge in North Korea is typical of the kind of interdiction mission that Task Force 77 aircraft took part in for over three years. The Panther's speed breaks, extended only seconds before, are now almost fully retracted against the fuselage. Below, bomb craters from previous attacks can be seen in the ice as well as the remains of a by-pass constructed across the now partially thawed river.

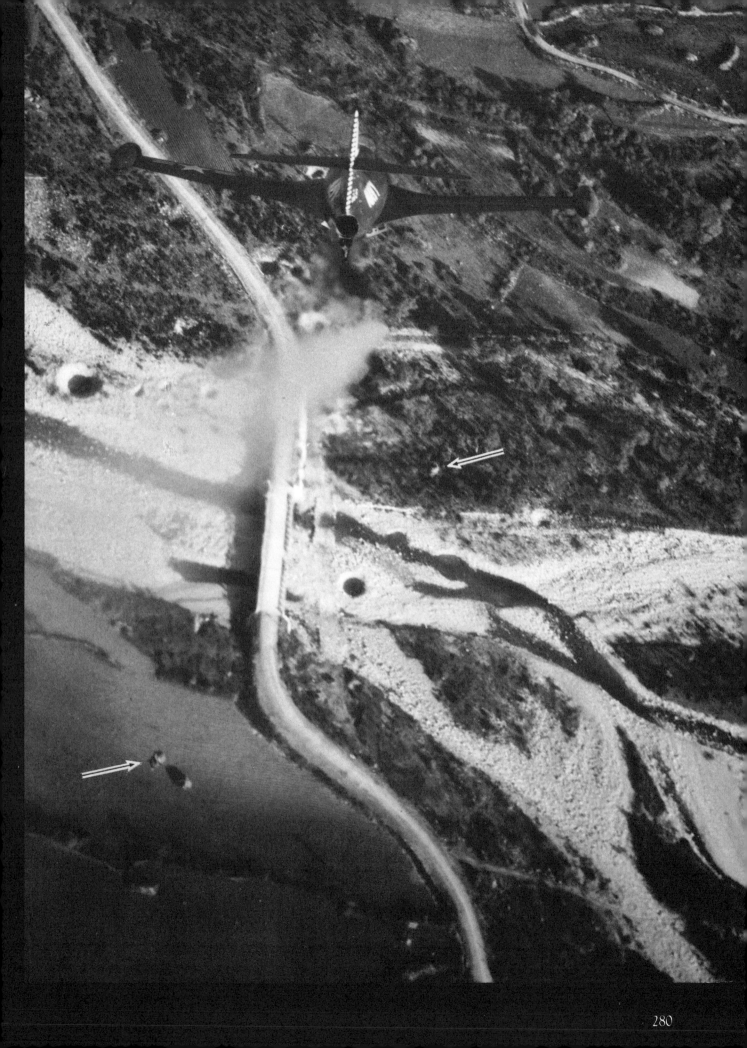

Carrier Airpower

A gull-winged F4U Corsair of the USS *Valley Forge's* Air Group 5 begins its takeoff roll, summer, 1950. These Corsairs are armed with eight 5-inch high-velocity rockets and one 150-gallon napalm bomb each. Although they are equipped to carry an additional napalm bomb under their port wings (which, with the other ordinance, would constitute a full *Baker* load), either the mission didn't call for more bombs or they were attempting to stretch out a dwindling supply of munitions. (**Opposite top** to **bottom**) An AD Skyraider carrying a truely prodigious load of ten 250-pound fragmentation bombs and a 150-gallon napalm bomb gets a "go" signal from the launch director; A Firefly attack aircraft taking off fron the HMS *Glory*, June, 1951; a trio of F9F Panthers aboard the USS *Bon Homme Richard* named after the photo-journals *LIFE*, *PIC* and *Look*; and deck crew aboard the HMS *Ocean* awaiting word to remove the chocks bracing a revved-up Sea Fury fighter-bomber, March, 1953.

The F2H Banshee was similar in appearance to the Panther but had a more slender body, twin exhausts that emanated at the wing roots instead of the rear of the fuselage and a tail which jutted up at a sharp incline instead of a gradual slope. Although the Banshee was a slightly larger aircraft, it actually took up considerably less deck space than a Panther because its wings could be fully retracted (*see page 295*).

(**Opposite top**) The stern 8-inch guns of the heavy cruiser USS *Toledo* firing in support of ROK troops in the P'ohang-dong area, Tuesday, 22 August 1950. (**Opposite bottom**) 16-inch guns of the battleship USS *Missouri* blasting the North Korean port of Ch'ongjin on Thursday, 12 October, and (**below**) the *Missouri* paying a return visit on Sunday, 21 October. Located just 39 miles from the Soviet border, Ch'ongjin was a frequent target of Seventh Fleet bombardment groups. (**Above**) The premature detonation of a phosphorous shell from the battleship USS *New Jersey* shoots fiery trails over coastal installations near Hungnam, January, 1951.

While Air Force Superfortresses flying from Japan and Okinawa certainly did do a bang-up job of pummelling North Korean industrial targets, the huge Wonsan oil refinery was destroyed by Corsairs and Skyraiders from the USS *Valley Forge* on Tuesday, 18 July 1950, and not by B-29s, as was widely reported at the time and is even stated on the photograph's accompanying caption. (**Opposite top**) A Panther jet awaits the signal to take off from the USS *Philippine Sea* on Friday, 4 August, shortly after the ship joined Task Force 77. (**Opposite bottom**) Sea Furys streak past the British carrier HMS *Glory* shortly before she was relieved by the Australian HMAS *Sidney*, October 1951.

Commando raids along North Korea's coasts by ROK and British Marines were a regular feature of the naval war. The Communists conducted raids as well and made serious attempts to wrestle control of several offshore islands in the Yellow Sea from the South Koreans. (**Above**) British Royal Marine commandos disembarking from US Marine amtracks eight miles south of Songjin where they destroyed a stretch of railroad track in April, 1951. (**Opposite top**) The commandos planting demolition charges beneath the track and (**opposite bottom**) the final preparations to blow the line.

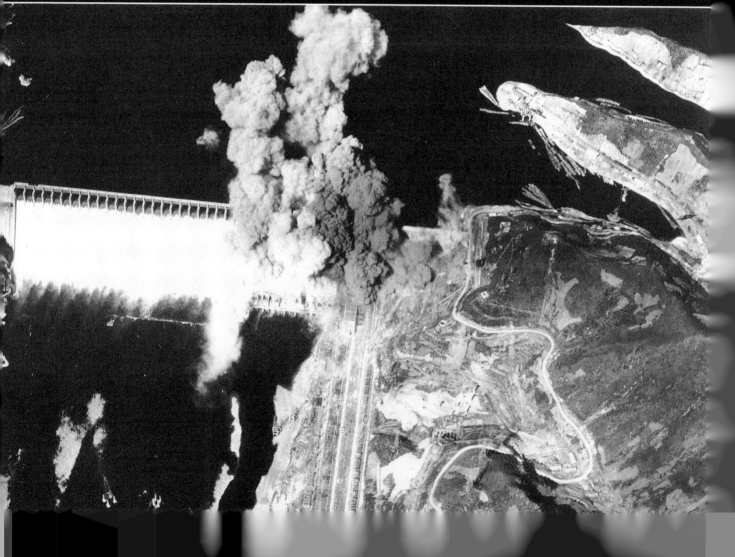

(**Opposite top**) An F9F Panther on an armed reconnaissance flight from the USS *Boxer* takes a look at the damage done to a Communist airbase at Sandok, Friday, 23 May 1953. The thickly cratered field had been repeatedly bombed during the extended— and successful— effort to keep Chinese MiG-15 jets from being based in North Korea. (**Opposite bottom**) Explosions rock the important hydroelectric generating facility at Suiho on the Yalu River, Monday, 23 June 1952. The carriers *Princeton*, *Boxer* and *Philippine Sea* provided 35 AD Skyraiders, each carrying one 1,000 and two 2,000-pound bombs, for the attack on the complex plus an additional 36 F9F Panthers, armed with 250-pound bombs, for flak suppression. A massive umbrella of 84 F-86 Sabres provided top cover against any intruding MiGs and aircraft from the *Bon Homme Richard* struck other hydroelectric plants. (**Above**) An HO3S-1 lands on the USS *Boxer* after a rescue mission, Wednesday, 12 September 1951.

Throughout the war, Japan was a forward staging area and re-source base of inestimable value. (**Left**) Laborers loading gasoline aboard an LST at Sasebo, Yokohama dock workers stand by as an Army truck is hoisted aboard a cargo ship and (**above**) crewmen of the battleship USS *Iowa* loading explosive charges for 5- and 16-inch projectiles at a southern Japanese port.

The destroyer USS *Stickell* and heavy cruiser USS *Helena* are refueled at sea by a Navy oiler, January 1953. (**Opposite**) An HO3S-1 rescue helicopter lands aboard the hospital ship USS *Consolation* with Marine casualties, Thursday, 24 January, 1952. The *Consolation* was anchored about two miles off shore from the town of Sokcho-ri, just above the 38th Parallel, and received 245 badly wounded patients from front-line aid stations during the holiday season of 1951 and first week of January 1952. The ship's helicopter landing platform had been built during the previous summer.

Snow squalls and ice on decks played havoc with flight operations during the long winters. Flight decks had to be repeatedly swept clean and jet exhausts had to be used to melt thick ice encrustations. Heavy seas, high winds and snow could prevent flight operations for days and, once launched, aircraft might have to be diverted to a land base if severe weather closed in again. (**Opposite**) Essex class carriers in the Sea of Japan; their flight operations suspended because of a dangerous coating of snow. The appearance of F2H Banshees parked along the port side of the deck indicates that the photos were taken during the second or third winters of the war. (**Above**) Unlike the shovel-armed deck crew in the bottom photo, the sailors aboard this Commencement Bay-class carrier, either the USS *Sicily* or USS *Badoeng Strait*, get a little help from a mechanical friend. Unfortunately, the snow flakes are coming down faster than man and machine can get rid of them as the successively whiter strips to their left show. (**Left**) During a snowstorm, William J. Lawton of the USS *Philippine Sea* primes a Corsair's engine by pulling its prop, Friday, 17 November 1950.

A rough landing on the deck of a Task Force 77 carrier ruptured the external belly tank of this AD Skyraider. Almost immediately, escaping fuel was ignited by the aircraft's hot engine exhaust. The pilot is hopping from the starboard wing while, in front of the port wheel, sailors are operating a fire extinguisher to help contain the blaze. Above them on the wing, another crewman is hurriedly yanking belts of 20-mm. ammunition from the gun bays before they begin to "cook off" from the raging fire. Although two fire teams are already in place with hoses, the water has yet to be turned on. The accident occurred in early November, 1952, and the aircraft carrier is either the USS *Oriskany* or USS *Kearsarge*.

(**Above**) A landing signal officer on the stern of the USS *Antietam* guides an approaching aircraft in for a safe landing; (**right**) an *Antietam* ordinanceman chats with a buddy while attaching detonating mechanisms to bombs mounted on an F4U Corsair; and (**below**) officers and men on the carrier's island superstructure observing flight operations. The ship's bridge is located behind the windows at the photo's center left.

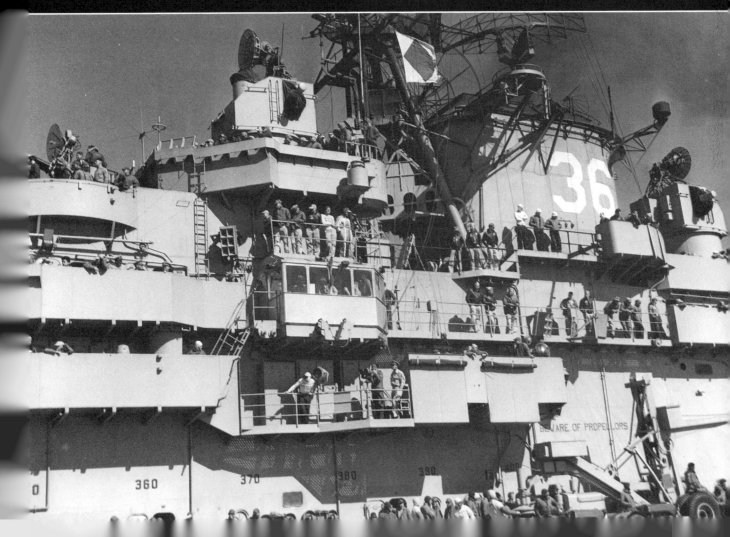

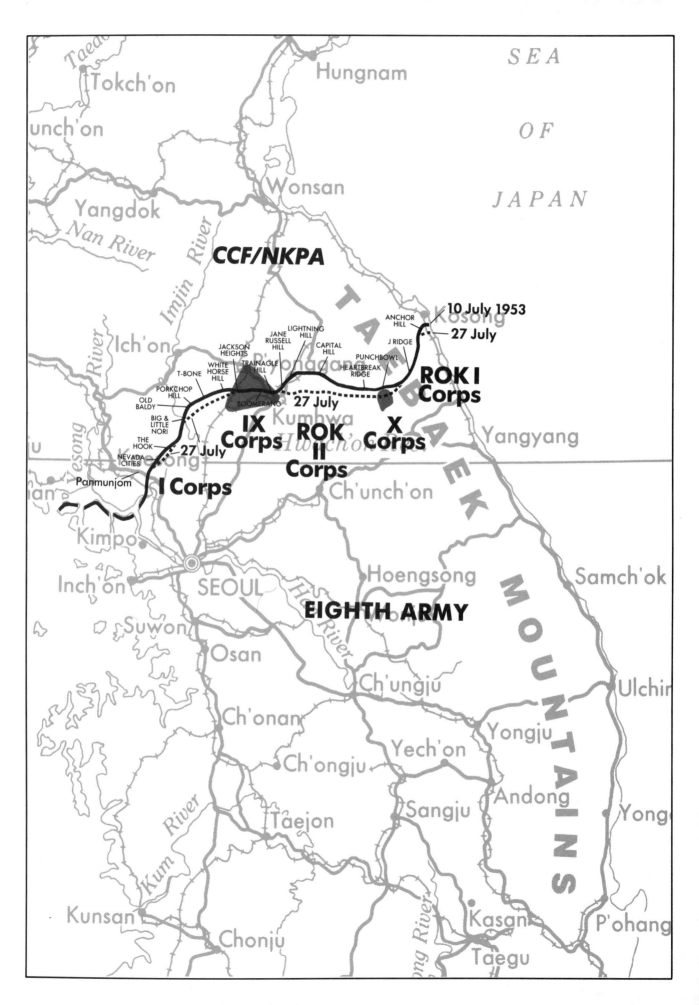

CHAPTER TEN

The Last Battles

The opening months of 1953 witnessed only the usual round of patrols, raids and ambushes across the frozen Korean landscape but, on the diplomatic front, there was discernible, if tentative, movement toward an end to the fighting. As the war dragged into its third winter, both sides wanted to put an end to it and the perception was growing in Washington and Tokyo that an honorable peace might be achievable in the near future if pressure were kept on the North Korean and Chinese economies.

In his 1952 presidential campaign, Dwight D. Eisenhower repeatedly pledged "I will go to Korea" and the President-elect fulfilled his promise with an uneventful, four-day tour of the battlefield in early December. As a practical matter, though, there was little he could do that had not already been done by the Truman administration. The break in the deadlock came when the Chinese suddenly accepted General Clark's renewed proposal that sick and wounded prisoners be exchanged.

The great demands of the war were draining China's weak economy and hindering its much-publicized, five-year industrialization plan. At a September 1953 meeting in Moscow, the Chinese Foreign Minister, Chou En-lai, tried unsuccessfully to persuade premier Joseph Stalin to further increase Soviet military and economic aid. After Stalin's death on 5 March 1953, Communist leaders apparently reviewed his confrontational policies and the new Soviet premier, Georgi Malenkov, spoke in favor of "peaceful coexistence" between the Communist and capitalist worlds.

Not only was the proposal to exchange the sick and wounded now accepted after numerous earlier rejections, but the larger question of a general POW exchange ap-

peared to be on its way to a settlement. Most of the agenda items discussed by the Communist and UN representatives had been cleared up early on in the negotiation process. However, the issue of what to do with each others prisoners had stalled any additional progress since the spring of 1952, when it was discovered that less than half of the 132,000 North Korean and Chinese prisoners wished to be returned to the Communists.

When the Communists learned the results of the International Red Cross prisoner screening, they immediately walked out of the truce talks, leveling charges of UN duplicity, and did not moderate their position for fifteen months. In effect, the roughly 375,000 casualties suffered by both sides between April 1952 and the end of the war (including more than 15,000 American dead and wounded) were the result of the United States' and the United Nations' refusal to force these prisoners to return to a life under Communist domination. It was not until after Stalin's death that the Chinese leadership decided there was some merit to an earlier Indian proposal that prisoners be turned over to a neutral nation; and they adopted it as their own. Once the prisoners were in neutral custody, representatives from the POWs' native countries could then try to convince them to return home during a period of "explanations," but could not force them to do so.

Events began to move swiftly. On 28 March, North Korean premier Kim Il Sung and Chinese commander in chief Peng Teh-huai agreed to Clark's proposal for an immediate exchange of the sick and wounded and, in an orchestrated response three days later, Kim accepted the "new" Chinese proposal on a general prisoner exchange. Communist liaison officers at Panmunjon asked that arrangements for the initial exchange be made quickly and, at a series of meetings from 6 to 11 April, the details were worked out in a brisk, business-like manner. The 20 April repatriation of sick and wounded POWs, dubbed Operation *Little Switch*, proceeded smoothly and three days later, UN Command representatives met with the Communists and agreed to reopen full plenary sessions on 26 April, the last Sunday of the month.

The negotiations were now proceeding at a breathtaking pace but, along the I Corps' front, the fighting returned to the familiar deadly pattern. The last week of March contained some of the most vicious combat of the war as seesaw battles raged across Old Baldy, Eerie and Porkchop Hill, held by the 7th Infantry Division and its Colombian battalion; as well as the Marines' "Nevada Cities" outposts of Carson, Reno, Elko and Vegas on a series of low hills 25 miles to the southwest.

Heavy fighting again erupted in this area at the end of May. The CCF struck the Nevada Cities complex and the adjacent outposts of Berlin and East Berlin, defended by the 25th Infantry Division's Turkish Brigade, and the Hook in the British Commonwealth Division's sector. In fierce, hand-to-hand battles along the trench lines, the Turks resisted all attempts to eject them from several outposts but were finally driven from Carson. With the help of a US battalion operating under Turkish command, a mixed force at Elko managed to repulse six Chinese assaults which often advanced to within grenade-throwing range. The Turks and Americans were eventually pulled off Vegas and Elko when the UN Command determined that the CCF was determined to seize the outposts at any cost and that the price of holding them far outweighed their value of delaying attacks on the MLR. On the exposed Hook, guarding the Samich'on Valley, British bunkers and trenches were smashed almost flat by a massive bombardment and forward positions were overrun. Only the timely arrival of reinforcements managed to keep the Hook in UN hands. Meanwhile, in the IX Corps area to the east, the ROK Capital and 9th Divisions also withstood tremendous poundings by Chinese mortars and artillery as they repulsed regimental sized attacks.

Continuous and extensive movement of enemy troops in late May and early June made it clear that the Communists were preparing themselves for their first major offensive in over two years. The armistice was nearly ready to be signed and any dents they could make in the MLR would become a permanent part of the final demarcation line bisecting the peninsula. The Chinese also wanted to inflict as much pun-

ishment as possible on the Republic of Korea's army.

The agreement negotiated at Panmunjon left Korea divided into Communist and non-Communist halves. To South Korean President Syngman Rhee, this was intolerable. He flatly refused to become a party to any agreement which returned the country to the *status quo* of 1950 and demanded that the war be pursued to final victory. The Chinese wanted to teach the obstinate president a lesson and General Clark later commented: "There is no doubt in my mind that one of the principal reasons— if not the one reason— for the Communist offensive was to give the ROKs a bloody nose; to show them and the world that *Puk Chin*— Go North— was easier said than done."

The ROK II Corps, occupying the northward bulge in the UN lines facing Kumsong, was struck by the full weight of three CCF armies on the night of Friday, 10 July. But if the Chinese hoped to send the South Koreans reeling back in disarray, as they so often had in the past, they must have been greatly disappointed. In spite of many deficiencies in the ROK army, the long years of training and battlefield experience had paid off. Portions of the front broke under the crushing weight of the assault but gaps were successfully plugged and a new MLR was established when the offensive lost steam only a week after it had begun. The CCF had expended some 7,000 men to push the South Koreans back only 4,000 yards.

Syngman Rhee's response to the Chinese onslaught, and what he believed was his deteriorating political position, was to try to torpedo the armistice negotiations. He very nearly succeeded. On 18 June, Rhee's military police released 27,000 North Korean POWs who had stated their unwillingness to be repatriated. As expected, the Communist negotiators immediately stormed out of the truce talks and, on 24 June, initiated fierce local attacks at ROK positions all along the front. On 1 July, the 40th and 45th Infantry Divisions began repositioning westward toward the Hwach'on Reservoir area to bolster the right flank of the ROK II Corps and both the 24th Infantry Division and 187th Airborne Regimental Combat Team in Japan were ordered back to Korea.

I Corps positions north of the Imjin River were attacked on Monday, 6 July, and part of Porkchop Hill was invested by the Chinese. After several days of fighting in which neither side could dislodge the other, the 7th Infantry Division's soldiers were taken off the hill because the number of casualties likely to be suffered retaining Porkchop were not worth its tactical value, especially since it was slated to be within the 4-kilometer wide Demilitarized Zone between

A sign in front of the Hant'an River bridge on Road 3 cautions jeep and truck drivers that the area beyond is under enemy observation, Wednesday, 21 January 1953. Road 3 was the main supply line to 25th Infantry Division troops in the Kumhwa area.

the opposing armies. To the southwest, the 1st Marine Division returned to their old positions on 7 July when they relieved the 25th Infantry Division. Since the Nevada Cities outposts had been lost in the interim, the line was much weaker than when they defended the area in March. Chinese infantry repeatedly attacked the remaining outposts, Berlin and East Berlin, and were driven back by the Marines and Turkish troops. At one point in the two days of hand-to-hand fighting on East Berlin, Marines literally hurled Chinese soldiers down the hill's reverse slope.

The Communists returned to the bargaining table on Friday, 10 July, after UN Command representatives assured them that the Republic of Korea would abide by the terms of an armistice. Rhee's support had been secured by the Eisenhower administration's offer of a mutual security pact and long term economic aid, starting with a $200,000,000 down payment on an expansion of the Republic's army to 20 divisions.

On the night of 13 July, the front erupted in one last convulsion of fighting as the Chinese renewed their effort to secure a final battlefield victory against the South Korean army; a propaganda victory which would allow them to claim that they had forced the "Yankee imperialists' running dog lackies" to sue for peace. The bulge facing Kumsong was again the main focus of the CCF's effort and some ROK units were cut off by penetrations in the Capital and 6th Division's fronts. Both divisions retired slowly while

taking a heavy toll on the attacking Communists. The ROK 3d and 8th Divisions to their right also withdrew under pressure.

The 3d Infantry Division, which had taken a hand in repulsing the previous month's offensive, realigned itself to cover the ROK Capital Division's left flank while the 2d Infantry Division extended its sector to the right to cover some of the positions vacated by the 3d. The balance of the 3d's old positions were filled by the 187th Airborne Regimental Combat Team and a regiment of the 24th Infantry Division. The latter had rushed up from Pusan and positioned itself behind the 2d where it could counterattack the flank of any enemy breakthrough. The Chinese assault subsided after several days and the reinforced ROK II Corps drove forward to retake the high ground along the Kumsong River. All of its objectives were seized by Sunday, 19 July, but no determined effort was made to move north and recover its original line since agreement had just been reached on all armistice terms. The front settled down to minor patrolling as the 27 July signing date neared but, in a move to gain control of the Imjin River, the Chinese made one last grab at the Marine positions in I Corp's sector.

The Berlin and East Berlin outposts had been overrun even as the truce talks were being completed, and on the night of Friday, 24 July, the Chinese attacked the MLR itself. In the early days of June, before it was evident that the CCF intended to batter the South Koreans, General Clark and the new Eighth Army commander, General Maxwell D. Taylor, feared that the coming offensive would be aimed at UN positions above the Imjin River where the terrain allowed little defense in depth. If the Communists could pry the 1st Marine Division off Boulder City (Hill 119), I Corps would be forced to withdraw to the next series of hills and, under the terms of the armistice, this would cost UN forces the unfettered control of the river.

Fighting raged all through Saturday and well into the following morning along 700 yards of front line trenches and at outposts Esther and Dagmar. After a relatively quiet Sunday, two final lunges were made at Boulder City that night but the Marines refused to be dislodged. At 10:00 am the following morning, Monday, 27 July 1953, representatives from both sides affixed their signatures to nine maroon-colored copies of the settlement for the Communist delegation and an equal number of blue-bound copies for the United Nations. Twelve hours later the cease-fire went into effect. The war in Korea was over.

Despite the severe cold, UN forces took advantage of the winter lull in fighting by taking some extra time to both relax as well as engage in training exercises designed to keep its fighters' skills from eroding. (**Above**) 1st Marine Division troops warm themselves by a small fire while waiting to move out at the Marines' tank-infantry school. (**Opposite**) British tankers have some tea and chat with an American soldier beside their Centurion and US Marine replacements being assigned to their new units.

A Marine rifle squad manages to stay dry by crossing a small river on the back of an M46 Patton. (**Below**) A wounded soldier is carried down from a hill position to a H-13 Sioux helicopter sheltered behind the reverse slope. Note the steps of loose rock held in place by staked branches. (**Opposite**) Canadian troops and Korean laborers work their way up a steep hill in the British Commonwealth Division's sector.

Once the frontlines had stabilized in 1951, the Republic of Korea and United Nations Civil Assistance Command began to make some headway towards working out the country's severe refugee problem. By the end of the war, some semblance of normalcy was actually beginning to return to Korean society. (**Above**) A mother with a baby strapped to her back receives an inoculation from Dr. Cho who is treating the people of her village with medicines provided by the 2d Infantry Division's Civil Assistance Office, March 1952. (**Opposite top**) Korean orphans enjoying a Roy Rogers comic book. The tiny boots worn by the center youngster were donated by Mrs. John H. Samford of Birmingham, Alabama. (**Opposite bottom**) The Shin In Won orphanage in Pusan, Korea. The thousands of homeless children wandering amoung the refugees were rounded up and cared for in hundreds of small orphanages dotting the countryside and neighboring islands. Many Eighth Army units "adopted" nearby orphanages and helped support them with donations of money, clothing, food and other necessities.

(**Right**) Sergeant Sadri Ulke of the Turkish Brigade's heavy mortar company keeping in contact with an air observer plotting fire directions for his unit. (**Opposite**) 25th Infantry Division soldiers of the 2d platoon, L Company, 14th Infantry Regiment, clean their weapons after a night patrol. (**Below**) Flashes show Chinese and friendly positions during a night action at a US outpost. The forces indicated by the first and fifth circles are in direct contact. Note the sandbagged positions along the hilltop trench in the foreground. The other photos also show fortifications common to Korea's positional warfare and the eroding pathway in front of the 25th Division bunker is marked with strands of communication wire to help minimize unscheduled tumbles down hill.

Friendly fire on enemy positions

Friendly flares

Enemy artillery in valley

Enemy fire on friendly lines

Enemy artillery

Enemy mortar positions

310

The 2d Field Artillery Battalion of the 40th Infantry Division fires a salvo of 4.5 rockets at Chinese positions. The 24-tube T66 rocket launcher was capable of firing 96 rounds every five minutes. (**Opposite**) A Marine helicopter insertion of a T66 battery. (*Clockwise from upper left*) The battery is *a*, dropped into place; *b*, positioned; *c* and *d*, loaded and aimed; *e* fired; and *f*, hooked up and wisked away before the Chinese can target and strike the position with their artillery.

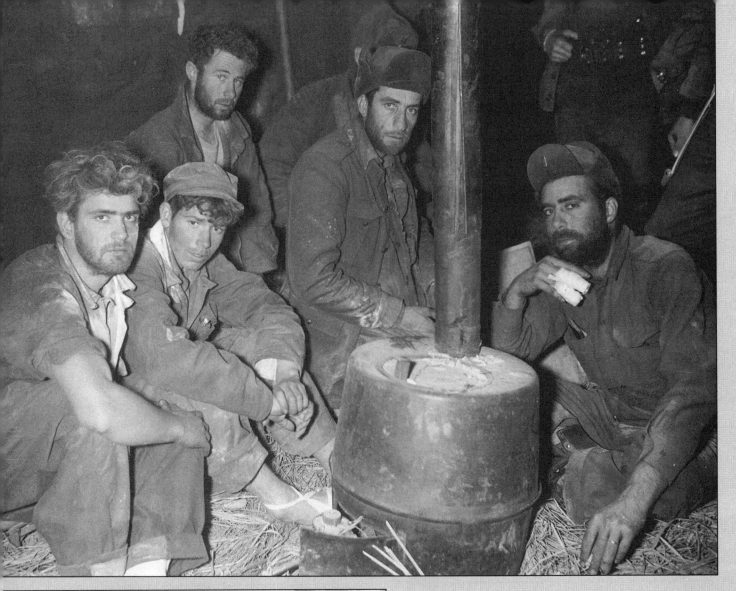

The widespread and well-documented murders of US and South Korean prisoners by North Korean Communists in 1950 received worldwide attention. The Red Chinese believed that this bad press severely damaged their cause by undermining the Communist's relations with both neutral and combatant nations; put their representatives at a disadvantage in various international forums including the UN; and stiffened the will of UN forces to fight long and hard on the battlefield. Consequently, the major focus of the Communist's propaganda effort along the portions of the front held by US and British Commonwealth troops was directed at convincing them that it was safe to surrender.

During the fluid warfare of early 1951, several small groups of prisoners who were having trouble keeping up with the retreating Chinese were released instead of being shot. (**Above**) American and Australian soldiers at a 24th Infantry Division medical station after reaching US lines and (**left**) one of 12 freed Americans who staggered into British Commonwealth Division positions, February, 1951. These releases were often referred to in Chinese surrender leaflets (**opposite left**). Simple, well-written safe conduct passes were common (**opposite right**) but usually had any potential effectiveness negated by looney messages on the reverse that were produced by propagandists who assumed that US soldiers held the same world view as the Communists. More sophisticated efforts (**opposite bottom**) were produced near the end of the hostilities.

跟我們走保證你的安全
FOLLOW US! WE GUARANTEE YOUR SAFETY

1. 我們將你送到後方安全的地方去。
   We will take you to a safe place in the rear.

2. 在我們的後方有你們成千的伙伴，他們過着安全愉快的生活，到後方後你就可以看到他們。
   Thousands of your fellow soldiers are in the rear. They have peace and safety. You will see them soon.

3. 我們志願軍不傷害俘虜，不虐待俘虜，不要俘虜私人的東西，這是我們的紀律。
   We Chinese Volunteers do not harm, and do not maltreat war prisoners, nor do we take any of their personal belongings. These are our regulations.

4. 你受傷了嗎？我們有人給你醫治。
   If you are wounded, you will get medical treatment.

5. 你可以寫信給你家裏報告你平安的消息。
   You will be able to write home and tell your folks you are safe.

6. 我們已經釋放了很多英美俘虜，你們將來也一定得到釋放。
   We have already set free many American and British prisoners. You will certainly be freed and get home in the end.

THE CHINESE PEOPLE'S VOLUNTEER FORCES
（發給每一個戰士，備捉俘虜後用）

Korea's where the GI's die,
Home's where the politicians lie.
**YOU RISK YOUR LIFE,
BIG BUSINESS RAKES IN THE DOUGH.**

REVERSE

FRONT

SAFE CONDUCT PASS
We guarantee:
If you put down your weapon and say

投 *TOW SHONG* 降
(surrender)
TOW rhymes with SHOW
SHONG rhymes with LONG

You will be escorted to the rear—to safety. You will get medical treatment if you need it. You will be well treated and, in the end, you'll get home in one piece.

THE CHINESE PEOPLE'S VOLUNTEER FORCES

SAFE CONDUCT PASS
安 全 通 行 證
통 행 증
中國人民志願軍司令部發
THE CHINESE PEOPLE'S
VOLUNTEERS' HEADQUARTERS

They smile because they are safe and happy with us.

Other types of leaflets preying on the fear of death, concern for loved ones, and hate for "war profiteers."

Mr. Moneybags is in Florida this Christmas.

Where are you? In Korea!

You risk your life, Big Business rakes in the dough.

傳單 － 117

USE YOUR HEAD, SOLDIER!

If You Want to Keep It!

Associated Press reported from Seoul, October 8:

"North Korean artillery fired 39,000 rounds within 24 hours ending 6 o'clock October 7. Soldiers were pinned down for long hours in the trenches and bunkers by enemy fire which continued for days and nights."

Hanson Baldwin, *New York Times* military commentator wrote June 12:

"Superiority on the battlefront, which the UN had a year ago, has now moved to the enemy side."

U.S. News & World Report wrote June 21:

"U.S. air superiority in Korea is no longer absolute."

EVERY G.I. THAT'S BEEN IN BATTLE KNOWS THE SCORE:

● Bullets and shells hit everything above ground. He's smart to get in a hole and stay there.

● To go out on patrol is the best way to get killed. Don't do it.

● The first man forward in an assault is the first man to get hit. What's the good of looking for death?

USE YOUR HEAD AND PLAY SAFE!

167

315

"Darling, I will dream that you are coming back to me this Christmas. I can't think of a Christmas without you."

Friday July 25th 1952 10.50 pm

Darling,

As I lie here in your room my thoughts are out there with you wherever you are. It may sound funny, and it's hard to understand, but no matter how far away, part of me will be there too. Darling since I've been home I've felt so close to you. Everytime I go to the closet to get a dress, and I see your suits and coats hanging in there, something comes over me and I get weak in my knees and I just have to stop a while and close my eyes. I guess it is all a part of being in love, and being separated from the one you love.

They wonder why I don't eat. In the first place I don't have the appetite, and haven't had much of an appetite for almost a year. Shall I tell you why? Yes baby, I know. Nothing will affect your appetite. But I'm different - you affect practically every part of me. They physical, mental and spiritual sides too.

Goodnight darling, I will dream you are coming back to me this Christmas. I can't think of a Christmas without you. I wish I could fall asleep tonight in your arms. Wouldn't we both be happy?

As Ever

157

A Soldier's Last Letter

Dear Mom,

I miss you so much, oh mom, I didn't know I loved you so, but I'll prove it when this useless war is over — I'm writing this letter in a foxhole, so don't scold me if it isn't so neat as I did when I was a kid & came home with mud on my feet. The Captain just gave us orders & mom we have to carry it through. I'll finish this letter the first chance I get but for now I'll just say I love you

This is an unfinished last letter received by an American mother from her son who was killed in Korea.

Soldiers! Don't get killed in this useless war. Don't let this happen to your dear mother at home who is praying day and night for your safety.

DEMAND PEACE, STOP THE WAR, so that you can go home and dispel the gnawing anxiety which is tearing your mother's heart.

144

The approach of summer brought heavy but sporadic fighting along the front. (**Above**) A blast which the Marine rifleman and photographer probably found too close for comfort. (**Opposite**) Patton tanks of the 7th Infantry Division firing at bunkers in the Ch'orwon Valley and Private Hans Hirsch of the 2d Infantry Division taking a much needed bath, Sunday, 24 May 1953.

An enemy bunker is destroyed by a satchel charge while (**below**) Private Gandana Sakuma and Corporal Tsegaie W. Yes of the 7th Infantry Division's Ethiopian Battalion mortar Chinese positions from outside their own bunker. (**Opposite top**) Tankers of the ROK 9th Division fire on Jane Russell Hill which had been lost in earlier fighting, Thursday, 21 May 1953, and (**opposite bottom**) a 1st Marine Division sniper fires on Communist soldiers on the next ridge.

A wounded 7th Divsion infantrymen is helped away from Porkchop Hill, Friday, 17 April 1953. (**Above right**) Members of the 25th Infantry Division's Turkish Brigade prepare to move out on a night patrol near Kumhwa. The Turks held tenaciously to the Nevada City outposts in May 1953 and again to the Berlin outposts in July. (**Below**) Major Charles E. Undercoffer, executive officer of the 7th Division's 73d Tank Battalion, directs an M46 Patton's fire against Chinese positions near Porkchop Hill, Sunday, 11 July.

A searchlight position on a road carved across a hill near Ch'orwon. This area was held by the 45th Infantry Division's Philippine Battalion and a quad-50 can be seen further up the road. (**Below**) A 7th Infantry Division checkpoint behind the MLR is flooded by monsoon rains during the Porkchop Hill fighting, Tuesday, 7 July 1953. A pair of the division's new M59 armored personnel carriers are at right. They carried supplies to contested outposts and, on Sunday, 11 July, were used to pull troops off Porkchop.

By the end of the fighting in Korea, the Republic of Korea's armed forces had grown from a pre-war strength of less than 100,000 to over 590,000 men. It was a battle-hardened force that acquitted itself well during the last mammoth Chinese offensives in June and July of 1953. (**Above**) an ROK infantryman with an M20 3.5-inch rocket launcher and (**right**) Major Odel Ferrell of the Korean Military Advisory Group (*at top with glasses*) supervises a class of artillery students at the Korean Army Training Center. (**Opposite top**) Officers and men of the 11th ROK Division and officials of the Korean Military Advisory Group watch a tactical demonstration by an ROK battalion, March 1952. (**Opposite bottom**) Sergeant William Givan instructs soldiers of the ROK 3d Division as they dry fire M1 Garand rifles, October 1951.

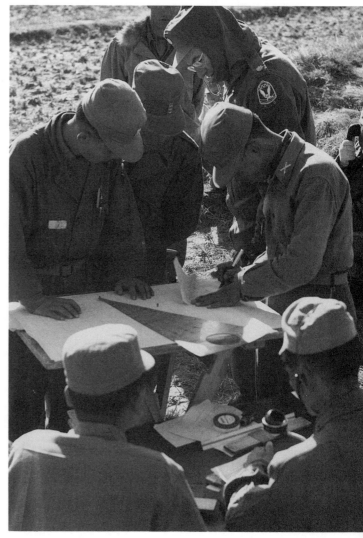

Monday, 27 July 1953: With the sounds of artillery fire still thundering throughout the surrounding I Corps area, American officers (**top**) examine the Armistice papers and exchange them with their Communist counterparts across the table. (**Above**) After 18 million words spoken at 575 regular meetings, the chief negotiators, Lieutenant Generals Nam II (*right*) and William K. Harrison sign the truce agreement at 10:00 am. Twelve hours later the cease fire went into effect. (**Right**) The commander-in-chief of all UN forces, General Mark W. Clark, countersigns the Armistice documents at Munsan-ni as the naval forces commander, Vice Admiral Robert P. Briscoe, looks on.

Sergeant Harry Sherman (*left*) and Private Roy Zehren help a wounded soldier down to an aid station near Old Baldy.

The last day of the war saw almost no ground activity other than extremely heavy artillery fire. UN aircraft continued their campaign to block Communist resupply efforts and, in the Sea of Japan, the US Navy ended the longest naval seige in history with a final bombardment of Wonsan. Air strikes and artillery fire continued into the night but at 10:00 the guns fell silent across the front and the last B-26 bomber had pulled out of North Korean airspace.

Between March 1952 and May 1953, six US combat divisions were withdrawn from the Republic of Korea as 200,000 Communist troops returned to China. The 40th and 45th Infantry Divisions of the National Guard were the first units to leave; the 1st Marine Division was the last. (**Right**) Troops boarding a Liberty ship for the trip home and (**below**) impatient soldiers waiting for their ship to dock in San Francisco. The Golden Gate Bridge is faintly visible in the distant mist. (**Opposite**) A sailor's homecoming in San Diego.

US Army infantrymen keeping watch along the Demilitarized Zone (DMZ) after the signing of the Armistice and (**opposite**) a soldier stands guard on Hill 119, Boulder City, where the Chinese troops last fought US troops. In 1971, nearly 26 years after it landed at Pusan to disarm Japanese troops, the 7th Infantry Division withdrew from the peninsula and the remaining US division on the DMZ, the 2d, was relieved by an ROK division and went into Eighth Army reserve. With the exception of the Joint Security Area for the Armistice Committee at Panmunjom, the entire 155-mile DMZ was now defended by the Republic's armed forces.

Today, the 2d Infantry Division, which fought at Wonju, Chip'yong-ni, the Pusan Perimeter, Heartbreak Ridge, and Kunu-ri— where it was nearly destroyed, is stationed in the Ch'orwon Valley on the main invasion route to Seoul. While US troop strength in the peninsula experiences periodic reductions and the Republic of Korea's highly developed armed forces are fully capable of defending their homeland, the US presence is viewed by South Koreans, Japanese and other East Asians as a stabilizing force in a part of the world whose Communist countries have yet to feel the changes experienced in Eastern Europe. The 2d is likely be in Korea for a long time to come.

Bibliography

The principal works I referred to the most when producing *War in Korea* were books produced under the auspices of the four armed services from the mid 1950s through the early 1960s. Although they may at first glance appear dated, they remain a superb source of basic information on the Korean War and later, more colorful books released by commercial publishers have borrowed freely from these works. The five volume *US Marine Operations in Korea* (Washington, DC: USMC, 1954-1962); James A Field's *History of United States Naval Operations: Korea* (Washington, DC: USN, 1962); and Robert F. Futrell's *United States Air Force in Korea, 1950-1953* (Washington, DC: USAF, 1983 edition) are all definitive histories of these services operations.

From the Army, Roy E. Appleman's *South to the Naktong, North to the Yalu* (Washington, DC: USA, 1961) is a brutally honest account of its' unprofessional performance during the first five months of the Korean War and Walter G. Hermes' *Truce Tent and Fighting Front* (Washington, DC: USA, 1966) covers the last two years of the conflict from July 1951 through July 1953. The intervening eight months was to be covered in a work titled "Ebb and Flow," which was being put together as early as 1964 or 1965. In August, 1971, Charles B. MacDonald of the Office of the Chief of Military History informed *Military Review* that the history was "approximately half" finished but it has yet to be published. Although a brief official account of Army operations during this period can be obtained from *Korea 1950* and *Korea 1951-1953* (Washington, DC: USA 1952 and 1956 respectively), readers must go to General Matthew B. Ridgway's *The Korean War* (Garden City, NY:

Doubleday, 1967) and the recently released works by Appleman such as *Disaster in Korea, The Chinese Confront MacArthur* and *East of Chosin, Entrapment and Breakout in Korea, 1950* for more detailed treatments.

Other fine works used in the production of this book were Richard P. Hallion's *The Naval Air War in Korea* (Baltimore, MD: The Nautical and Aviation Publishing Company of America, 1986) and Volume 3 of *The Years of MacArthur* (Boston: Houghton Mifflin, 1985) by D. Clayton James, a determinedly evenhanded treatment of one of this century's most controversial figures.

Credits

About the Author

D. M. Giangreco is an editor for the U.S. Army's professional journal, *Military Review*, published by the Command and General Staff College at Fort Leavenworth, Kansas. Mr. Giangreco has written on such wide ranging subjects as the Falkland Islands sovereignty question and decentralization of the Soviet Air Force command and control structure for the *Kansas City Star* and other Capital Cities Communications publications. Mr. Giangreco has also authored *Roosevelt, de Gaulle and the Posts: Franco-American War Relations Viewed Through Their Effects on the French Postal System, 1942-1944*, an examination of coalition warfare which focuses on how one specific French governmental agency managed to continue functioning during the liberations of France and French North Africa, and *Airbridge to Berlin: the Berlin Crisis of 1948, its Origins and Aftermath*, with Robert E. Griffin, on the city's turbulent years from the end of World War I through today's "Gorbimania." He is currently working on *Warlord of Kontum: John Paul Vann, the CORDS Years*, a study of the pacification programs during the Vietnam War and "Vietnamization." Mr. Giangreco lives in Kansas City, Missouri.